GOD SPEAKS TO AN X-RATED SOCIETY

Are the Ten Commandments Still Valid?

Edited by
ALAN F. JOHNSON

MOODY PRESS

CHICAGO

© 1973 by
THE MOODY BIBLE INSTITUTE
OF CHICAGO

Library of Congress Catalog Card Number: 72-95024

ISBN: 0-8024-3023-6

Second Printing, 1973

Printed in the United States of America

Contents

CONTRIBUTORS

RALPH ALEXANDER, TH.D.
Associate Professor of Bible

STEVEN BARABAS, TH.D.
Professor of Theology

DONALD HAGNER, PH.D.
Assistant Professor of Bible

ARTHUR HOLMES, PH.D.
Professor of Philosophy

CHARLES HORNE, TH.D.
Associate Professor of Theology

MORRIS INCH, PH.D.
Professor of Bible and Apologetics

HERBERT JACOBSEN, PH.D.
Assistant Professor of Bible

ALAN F. JOHNSON TH.D.
Associate Professor of Bible

DONALD LAKE, PH.D.
Assistant Professor of Bible

MERRILL TENNEY, PH.D.
J. P. Williston Professor of Bible and Theology

ROBERT WEBBER, TH.D.
Associate Professor of Bible

Foreword

This book reflects both concern and conviction. The concern is well founded. Despite the persistent caricatures of law and order, few citizens are prepared to endorse conditions which make strolling in the park at night—or even on the streets—a dangerous exercise, which require exact fares on public transportation to avoid robbery, and which demand security measures at airports as the only known means to reduce hijackings. Consider also the fact that today the chief executive of one of the world's most powerful nations is drastically limited in his personal activities because of the potential threat to his life.

Clearly there is need of some kind of control, but that this should be only through an increase in police power is both unfortunate and ultimately unworkable. What is essential is a moral consciousness that is informed by a recognized and equitable set of principles or ideals. For too long we have been assured that such a standard is natural to human beings and only freedom is needed to permit adherence to it. The history of the twentieth century corroborates that of earlier eras in refuting this assertion. Man by his very freedom of action is so manifesting his sinfulness that it does not require the magnification of publicity to be recognized for what it is. Its effects are too pervasive and too damaging to be overlooked.

But it is one thing to recognize the problem and quite another to do something about it. The authors therefore have focused their concern on more than analysis or description. They have included in their perspective their convictions about the pertinence of God's commandments for our times.

5

Such convictions presume not only that God is self-revealing but also that He is morally and ethically sovereign. Moreover, His commandments form an objective basis for His judgments in holding man accountable for the way in which he responds to God's prescriptions.

To the community of Christians at Wheaton College, these messages on the Ten Commandments were calculated to do more than inform. They were to inspire a commitment that in turn would have its effect both personally and generally. We are convinced that the outworking of conformity to the revealed will of God enables the Christian to be, in his manner of life, an eloquent enunciation of the truth of the Holy Scriptures.

This, then, is the purpose of this volume. It is not merely a report of something that took place on the Wheaton campus. It is instead a sharing of a concern and a declaration of conviction in order that the degree of obedience to the commandments of God might be increased and the effect of such response extended more widely in our society. It is in the constructive response to these statements that the concern of the various authors will find fulfillment. To the extent that these convictions are shared and produce a community of obedience, God will be honored and His purposes advanced in our time.

HUDSON T. ARMERDING
President
Wheaton College

Introduction

Are the Ten Commandments for Today?

ALAN F. JOHNSON

Does God have any relationship with our contemporary "x-rated" society? Emphatically, yes. So say ten leading evangelical scholars in the following pages. In addresses originally given before the combined student body and faculty of Wheaton College, the Ten Commandments are expounded and seriously related to the issues and problems of today's world.

In recent media reports and literature, the inhumanity of man is heralded as a growing characteristic of our society. Writing in an article entitled, "Now We're Living in 'Age of Terror,' " columnist Harriet Van Horne deplores the increasing crime, drugs, divorce, and fear in our society, and talks about the new book, *Robopaths,* by Dr. Lewis Yablonsky. She says:

> A "robopath" is a human being who has become socially dead. Yablonsky sees more brute ugliness in modern man than most of us ever imagined. People are becoming so robot-like in their social interaction, he believes, that our social order will be permanently damaged if we do not recover our essential humanity.
>
> Americans have become so dehumanized this professor at a California state college writes, that many could be described as "the walking dead." We live in a world wired for death. And it's going to take enormous concerted effort by the good people to save us.[1]

We believe the root of the problem is moral and spiritual. In an age of moral permissiveness and spiritual darkness, men need to return to God and His law.

When we consider the major social problems flowing in our culture and realize their close relationship to these basic ten commands of God, we are again impressed with Moses' pertinence to our day. In the first few commands, the issue of man's central ideology or core of his existence is raised. Who or what will be our God? Man's identity, purpose, and meaning are established by these words. The essays of Dr. Tenney, Dr. Jacobsen, Dr. Webber, and Dr. Horne discuss the relevance of these commands to the contemporary problems of relativism, nihilism, humanism, despair, the silence of God, and secularism.

Modern day issues with respect to the family, abortion, war, capital punishment, euthanasia, and the new morality, find references in Dr. Alexander's and Dr. Holmes' treatment of the fifth and sixth commandments. With mounting pressure to alter drastically our society's marriage and divorce laws, Dr. Inch's timely discussion of the seventh commandment should be noted.

Finally, with the alarming increase in burglaries and theft of all types, with the serious credibility gap in the truthfulness of advertising and government, and with the problem of poverty in an affluent society, the discussions by Dr. Hagner, Dr. Barabas, and Dr. Lake prove again the perennial need of acknowledging the law of God within a society which is seeking stability.

The Ten Commandments (ten words), or the Decalogue, have been of inestimable importance for the development of history and contemporary religious and cultural life. Though still doubted by some, a growing number of biblical scholars are reaffirming the essential Mosaic authorship of the Pentateuch and the Ten Commandments.[2] Moses would have written about 1400 B.C.

With slight modifications on the Sabbath and coveting commands, the ten commands appear in two separate passages in the Pentateuch: Exodus 20:1-17 and Deuteronomy 5:6-21. They are viewed in these references as originating directly from God Himself as given in revelation to Moses.

It would be wrong to separate the first five commands from the last, since they constitute one law in the form of a covenant agreement between the Lord and His people. The first five commands establish their unique relationship to Him out of which the last five commands find their distinctive significance and can alone be realized. The words of the preamble of the covenant cannot be forgotten in understanding the significance of the "ten words": "I am the LORD your God, who brought you out of the land of Egypt, out of the house of slavery" (Ex 20:2). The Decalogue was the Magna Charta of freedom given to a divinely redeemed people who were committed to a new Master for their complete life-style. These words emphasized not only this nation's freedom, but also the sheer undeserved grace that lay behind their liberty. Because of this grace of God, they must learn to live not in the hope of attaining salvation by moral or religious striving, but in the gladness of a salvation already freely given by a God who knows all their weaknesses and the mayhem that their sinful, rebellious natures could work in His plans.

While parallels to the last five commands do exist in ancient Near Eastern legal literature before Moses' time (e.g., Hammurabi, c. 1700 B.C.; Ur-Nammu of Ur, c. 2050 B.C.), the differences are noteworthy. No ancient legal code was ever formulated in short, imperative, negative clauses as are the Mosaic commands, nor was any early code so entirely permeated with the religious bond as the Ten Commandments.[3] Consequently, the uniqueness of the commandments for Israel lay not in terms of a statement of some type of universal moral law or principles, but in the awareness that they were the rightful expectation of her Lord's claim upon them through redemption. Man today, likewise, does not need a new call to morals, but he needs a summons to a radically new relationship to God through redemption.

That the commands appear for the most part in a negative fashion demonstrates the utmost wisdom. As Mendenhall observes: "It has been pointed out that prohibitions only are universal, since they define only the areas which are not permitted, *leaving all other realms of action free.* A positive command, on the other hand, immediately excludes all other alternatives."[4] Thus the commands insure both man's obedience and his freedom in decision making.

Unfortunately no uniform numbering of the commands prevails either among the Jews or Christians. The main divisions are given in the following summary.

1. *Jewish divisions of the commands.* The opening words of the preamble are considered the first command, "I am the Lord thy God." The next two commands (no other gods and graven images) are combined into one and considered as the second commandment.

2. *Roman Catholic and Lutheran divisions.* Following the example of Augustine, the first two commands are merged into one and considered as the first commandment. In order to keep the total number ten, what is otherwise called the tenth commandment was divided, thus making the ninth and tenth commandments. This throws the numbering off from the Jewish and other Christian schemes. Furthermore, the Lutherans reverse the order of the ninth and tenth commands.

3. *Consensus view.* Following the ancient Jewish writers, Philo and Josephus, the early Christian writer—Origen, the Greek Orthodox, and all Protestant churches except the Lutherans, the first command begins with the first negative prohibition (no other gods) and the second with the next negative (no graven images). This view seems the most defensible. It avoids the unnatural splitting of the tenth command into a command against coveting the neighbor's wife,

which in effect makes it a duplication of the command against adultery, and a further general command against coveting other things. Rather, the whole tenth command concerns coveting. We have followed the Reformed (Calvinistic) divisions as being the most easily defensible system.

The contents of the first five commandments may be briefly described as follows: (1) against polytheism (many gods); (2) against idolatry in all forms; (3) against dishonoring of God's name; (4) on Sabbath observance; and (5) on honoring parents. With the exception of the last, these commands describe the relationship of the redeemed to God. The fifth command actually forms a transition between the responsibilities toward God and those toward others. Scripture views the raising of children as a sacred obligation to God Himself.

In the last five commands, the relationship to the other person in the whole social and ethical realm is stressed and may be described in short form as follows: (6) against taking human life; (7) against violation of the marriage union; (8) against violating the sanctity of property; (9) against false witness; (10) against envy and greed.

We should not study the Ten Commandments without considering the inspired interpretation of their intent given by Jesus and the apostles in the New Testament. Do not overlook the penetrating interpretation for the first century (A.D.) of a number of these commands as Christ lay bare their inward motivational nature (Mt 5:21-48) and their continued effectiveness (Mt 5:17-20). Do not fail to see how Jesus summed up the essence of the commands in two great commands: " 'YOU SHALL LOVE THE LORD YOUR GOD WITH ALL YOUR HEART, AND WITH ALL YOUR SOUL, AND WITH ALL YOUR MIND.' . . . And . . .'YOU SHALL LOVE YOUR NEIGHBOR AS YOURSELF' " (Mt 22:37, 39). And do not overlook Paul's insistence that all the commands are fulfilled or find their intent in loving the other person (Ro 13:8-10; Gal 5:14).

In our day an attractive and popular fallacy being perpetrated concerns the adverse relationship of God's law to love. Under various names, such as "the new morality" or "situation ethics," a dangerously inadequate view of Christian ethics is being advocated. You will especially want to read Dr. Holmes' treatment of the sixth commandment and Dr. Inch's remarks on the seventh commandment where they touch on this. Biblically speaking, love and God's law are complementary, not in opposition. The "love only" ethic fails to grasp the fact that not only is the context of love necessary in all our actions, but this love must find its content in the righteous standard of God which has been revealed in sacred scripture.

We also need to see these commandments against the historic interpretation of the law. According to Protestant understanding, three uses of the law are: a moral or religious use, a political use, and a didactic use. The moral use of the law refers to the guilt and condemnation which results when we see the holiness and perfection of God revealed in the law (Ro 7; Gal 3). The political use of the law is intended to bring order in society (Ro 13). Both Luther and Calvin, however, also taught a didactic use of the law. On the one hand the Ten Commandments are a demand of the holiness of God that is laid upon us; they are a demand which none of us can fulfill (Ro 3:19-20). By these commands we are shown to be sinners and under God's condemnation. Once we discover our inability to fulfill these commands, our true sinful condition becomes apparent. Seeing our need and our powerlessness to perform the good, we are driven to Jesus Christ to receive from God through faith the free gift of forgiveness and total acceptance (Ro 8). But once we are accepted by faith in Christ, these same Ten Commandments become the source of knowledge of God's will, and the way the Christian expresses his new life in Christ. This is the didactic (instructional) use of the law (Ro 13:8-10).

Finally, if the Ten Commandments are not highly pertinent to the reader's experience, may I suggest two possible reasons? Could it be that you have never personally entered into covenant relationship to God by receiving His free gift of forgiveness and deliverance offered through Jesus Christ? These commands only find their real meaning in the life of one who has trusted himself totally to the Redeemer God through Jesus Christ. Second, have you perhaps failed to realize that the commands of God are given through a specific time and culture which must be translated into our contemporary world? The principles embodied in these ten words are the never-changing will of God for His people, but they must be interpreted into our time and culture. This is what we believe the following pages will disclose.

The late G. Campbell Morgan aptly described the relevance of the Ten Commandments when he remarked, "He who lives without reference to the law of God fails to fulfill the possibilities of his own being. He is not a man until he lives by the words that proceed from the mouth of God."[5]

NOTES

1. Harriet Von Horne, "Now We're Living in an 'Age of Terror,' " *Chicago Today*, March 20, 1972.
2. R. K. Harrison, *Introduction to the Old Testament* (Grand Rapids: Eerdmans, 1970), pp. 80-82.
3. J. J. Stamm and M. E. Andrew, *The Ten Commandments in Recent Research* (Naperville, Ill.: Allenson, 1967), p. 33.
4. George E. Mendenhall, *Law and Covenant in Israel and the Ancient Near East*, p. 7. Johnson's italics. Quoted in *These Ten Words* by Roy L. Honeycutt (Nashville, Tenn.: Broadman, 1966), p. 13.
5. G. Campbell Morgan, *The Ten Commandments* (Chicago: Revell, 1901), p. 10. For further help on the commandments, see Ronald S. Wallace, *The Ten Commandments* (Grand Rapids: Eerdmans, 1965).

The Ten Commandments

1. You shall have no other gods before Me.
2. You shall not make for yourself an idol, or any likeness of what is in heaven above or on the earth beneath or in the water under the earth. You shall not worship them or serve them; for I, the LORD your God, am a jealous God, visiting the iniquity of the fathers on the children, on the third and the fourth generations of those who hate Me, but showing lovingkindness to thousands, to those who love Me, and keep My commandments.
3. You shall not take the name of the LORD your God in vain, for the LORD will not leave him unpunished who takes His name in vain.
4. Remember the sabbath day, to keep it holy. Six days you shall labor and do all your work, but the seventh day is a sabbath of the LORD your God; in it you shall not do any work, you or your son or your daughter, your male servant or your female servant or your cattle or your sojourner who stays with you. For in six days the LORD made the heavens and the earth, the sea and all that is in them, and rested on the seventh day; therefore the LORD blessed the sabbath day and made it holy.
5. Honor your father and your mother, that your days may be prolonged in the land which the LORD your God gives you.
6. You shall not murder.
7. You shall not commit adultery.
8. You shall not steal.
9. You shall not bear false witness against your neighbor.
10. You shall not covet your neighbor's house; you shall not covet your neighbor's wife or his male servant or his female servant or his ox or his donkey or anything that belongs to your neighbor.

Ex 20:3-17, as divided by Reformed Churches

14

The First Commandment

MERRILL C. TENNEY

EXODUS 20:3: *You shall have no other gods before Me.*

Of all the documents that have ever been written to lay down the principles of moral law, none has been more important for human health and happiness than the Ten Commandments. Transmitted through Moses at Mt. Sinai when the people of Israel were about to begin an independent national existence, these regulations express God's unchanging moral laws which apply to every generation of Jew and Gentile alike. They are not rules arbitrarily imposed upon some community by a sadistic tyrant, but are principles that are inherent in the constitution of the universe.

There is, of course, something about the word *commandment* that makes the hackles of our spines raise because we dislike coercion. Human nature tends to rebel against any expression of authoritarian rule. Nevertheless, we do not object to regulatory principles in the physical world. The scientist who does not respect the laws of chemistry may suddenly leave his laboratory via the roof. If one decides to jump from the top of the Washington Monument, he may be free to do so, but he cannot avoid landing on the ground with an inexpressibly sad crash. The principles of physics operate no matter what our choices or sentiments may be. The laws of the universe are inescapable, and we ignore them at our own peril.

Moral laws also exist. They inhere in the human nature of

man because he is a moral being. The Ten Commandments express them succinctly and very definitely.

These commandments were given by God to a people in the process of organizing. This unorganized rabble had just emerged from slavery where they had no privileges, no rights, no hope, and no future. God had delivered them from the grip of the strongest military nation of that period, had miraculously marched them through a wilderness where there was no food, and had assembled them before a mountain where He gave them, as the basic constitution of their future welfare, these ten words, as the Jewish people call them. Sinai was really a step in their education. God was providing the basis for their thinking and for their living in the new world which He expected them to create. These commandments, then, comprise two essentials: a revelation of truth and a demand for obedience.

The first commandment contains the revelation of the being of God. What is meant by the command: "You shall have no other gods before Me"? What is a god? God is not the product of a philosopher's speculation, nor a ghost raised by a superstitious imagination. He is the infinite person who is responsible for the creation, operation, and principles of the universe in which we live. He is not simply an impersonal force; nor is He an arbitrary despot. He is a person who loves us, who is deeply interested in our welfare, and who wants us to know Him.

On this particular occasion of the giving of the commandments, He disclosed Himself in three ways. First, He is a God of purpose. "I am the LORD your God, who brought you out of the land of Egypt, out of the house of slavery" (Ex 20:2). Why should He take them out of Egypt? Why remove them from a green and flourishing land into a barren wilderness? Why thrust them out of their homes into a nomadic existence? Why separate them from the acquaintances and the surroundings familiar to them to make them live among strangers? God had a purpose for them that transcended a mere existence in Egypt. Several hundred years earlier God had told their ancestor Abraham: "Know for certain that your descendants will be strangers in a land that is not theirs, where they will be enslaved and oppressed four hundred years. But I will also judge the nation whom they will serve; and afterward they will come out with many possessions" (Gen 15:13-14). God operates by the flow of the centuries; He may take a long time to develop His purpose, but He never fails to fulfill it. On this occasion, God had completed His purpose and had removed the people of Israel from bondage. The fact was well known to them; now, by the revelation of His law, God was explaining the outcome of that purpose. He wanted to make them a moral light to the nations, a model that the rest of the world could follow.

Second, He is a God of power. The God who should take first place in our lives is "able to do exceeding abundantly beyond all that we ask or think, according to the power that works within us" (Eph 3:20). The measure of God's power in any life is simply the measure of His command in that life. For the Israelites, Jehovah was the God of power. All the military might of Egypt availed nothing against these helpless people. When Pharaoh tried to recapture them, God opened the sea to make a path for their escape. God preserved them in a wilderness so barren that it grew no vegetation. God conducted them through numerous perils to their destination. The God whom we worship is not a God whom we have created; nor is He a limited God. He is rather the omnipotent God whose power is available for His people.

Third, Jehovah is a God of redemption. Not only is He able to formulate a purpose and competent to accomplish it, but He is also able to retrieve what is lost, to recreate what is broken, and to renew lives that are ruined. He is able to rescue men from their sins, shortcomings, and failures, and to bring them to Himself. Only He can restore a shattered reputation or remake a wrecked personality. Israel, spiritually impoverished by long decades of slavery, was reconstituted as a nation by the transforming power of God. For that reason, He can say, "You shall have no other gods before Me."

The word *redemption* has often become a theological cliché, but that does not empty it of truth. A cliché is simply a formula used so commonly that it has ceased to be impressive. Redemption means freedom instead of slavery, light instead of darkness, power instead of weakness. God gave Israel hope when they were despairing. When the genocide planned by the king of Egypt threatened them with extinction in one generation, God intervened and transformed a horde of helpless slaves into the instrument of His purpose for the world.

What does it mean to have such a God? The command is exclusive: "no other gods." Probably most people think of this injunction only in terms of polytheism. If they are not avowed worshipers of Brahma, Buddha, or Baal, and accompanying deities, they feel that they have kept the commandment quite satisfactorily.

The first commandment means, however, far more than a rejection of the many in favor of the one, and more than merely searching for reality. Its significance is not purely negative; it is positive. It presupposes absolute sovereignty, for the true God is not only the means of human existence, but also its end or goal. "All things have been created through Him and for Him" (Col 1:16). His sovereignty, moreover, is not something to be dreaded; God is not a policeman pursuing a criminal. His sovereignty means that He is able to control every avenue of life. He is able to take our careers and shape them to His own ends. His purpose will prevail whether we agree with it or not. We may choose to share in it and to partake of its benefits. The God whom we worship must become the ruler of our inner life that He may bend our hearts to do His will. He does not assume command of our destinies to enslave us but to empower us to become like

Himself. With the regulation comes renovation, so that we can echo the psalmist, who said, "I have inclined my heart to perform Thy statutes forever, even to the end" (Ps 119:112).

This attitude toward God leads directly to another implication of the commandment as expressed in Deuteronomy 6:5: "You shall love the LORD your God with all your heart and with all your soul and with all your might." The basic relationship between man and God is not an oppressive legalism, but is rather the fellowship that controls from within. Why should God take the primacy in life? Not because of a cold mechanical choice, nor because we have analyzed all other gods and have found them deficient, but rather because we love this God who has done so much for us. The Old Testament repeatedly asserts that the supreme manifestation of God's attitude toward His people was the deliverance from Egypt. He did for them what they could not rightfully demand from Him or compel Him to do, and what He had no apparent good reason to do. He has done the same for us. The mercies of God are founded solely on His goodness, not on human merit.

Probably few of us have ever bowed down physically before graven images of wood or stone, but we have all had our idols, whether they were persons, occupations, pleasures, or possessions. God requires our undivided affection; nothing less will satisfy Him. The New Testament emphasizes the principle when its says, "Guard yourselves from idols" (1 Jn 5:21).

Devotion, however, is not an emotional explosion, but voluntary dedication. The twentieth chapter of Exodus finds its real counterpart in Romans 12:1-2: "I urge you therefore, brethren, by the mercies of God, to present your bodies a living and holy sacrifice, acceptable to God, which is your spiritual service of worship. And do not be conformed to this world [age], but be transformed by the renewing of your mind, that we may prove what the will of God is, that which is good and acceptable and perfect."

To many, this application may sound restrictive and confining. To regard life as a continuous sacrifice, and to devote oneself singly to God seems like an unnecessary and unwelcome self-limitation. To make such a complaint is like a fish saying that the ocean is too small for him. The infinite God, with all His resources, with all of His wisdom, with all of His love, with all of the varied aspects of His character, and with all of the vast resources of the universe which He has created, can give us ample scope for exercising all our potentialities, satisfaction for all of our real desires, and direction to avert the waste of these resources.

Has anyone ever kept this commandment? The Lord Jesus Christ is the only one who can qualify perfectly. He recognized the purpose of God in His life, for He said, "I do not seek My own will but the will of Him who sent Me" (Jn 5:30). He fulfilled that purpose, for He prayed, "I glorified Thee on the earth, having accomplished the work which Thou hast given Me to do" (Jn 17:4). In all His life He obeyed perfectly the will of God, for He said: "I always do the things that are pleasing to Him" (Jn 8:29). Jesus is the perfect example of the meaning and fulfillment of the first commandment. He, living in us and working through us, provides the dynamic by which we can keep it.

The first commandment sets a standard for the spiritual life both by its requirements and by its implied fulfillment. God becomes the absolute answer to the relativism and nihilism of our age. He is by His own declaration purposeful, sovereign, loving, and redemptive. To worship Him as the only God commits us to Him in full trust and in an obedience that recognizes Him as the final authority for life. Such worship fixes the ultimate standards and destiny of those who acknowledge Him.

The Second Commandment

HERBERT JACOBSEN

EXODUS 20:4: *You shall not make for yourself an idol, or any likeness of what is in heaven above or on the earth beneath or in the water under the earth.*

The second commandment concerning the making of graven images is considered one of the simplest of the ten to understand. Once pronounced, it was followed soon after by a violation, namely, the actions of Aaron and the Jewish people in worshiping the golden calf (Ex 32). Two interpretations of the commandment stem directly from this experience, although both interpretations are inadequate.

One interpretation is that this commandment forbids idolatry. A good indication that the commandment does militate against idolatry is found in the phrase "worship them or serve them" (Ex 20:5). Occurring twenty-five times in the Old Testament, all but once it refers to worshiping and serving idols. This observation led the ancient church father Origen to comment that the commandment writes a merciless war on all other gods. But, if this view is true, it is not really a second commandment, for the first commandment forbids idolatry: "You shall have no other gods before me" (Ex 20:3).

The second interpretation, which seems a partial truth, is that the command forbids the use of images. Several persons throughout the Christian and Jewish traditions have suggested this. The Puritans, for example, never hung pictures in their homes. Others suggest it is irreligious to use a crucifix, or improper to have the stations of the cross in the church, or idolatrous to employ icons in worship. In this vein, G. Campbell Morgan mentions that several times in Westminster Abbey some of the statues of the saints were removed from their niches when the curators discovered these statues were being worshiped.[1]

In the first century this elimination of all forms was practiced as well. Some have tried to connect this aversion to artistic expression and the use of pictorial images with logograms. For example, in the Jewish tradition, the use of the mezuzah, a case containing Scripture attached to the doorpost, and in the Christian tradition the use of *icthus*, the symbol of the fish. But if this commandment forbids all kinds of images, then one is at pains to explain the absence of prophetic utterances against David and Solomon for the use of the cherubim in the temple and for the placing of lions at the entrance to the palace. These men surely did not violate the commandment. The first-century Jewish theologian Philo claims that Jews forbade the use of images only after an extremely literalistic interpretation of this commandment took over Judaism.

But clearly a sense of aversion to images exists in this commandment. In at least three specific areas, the Jews, for example, have built fences around their law to protect themselves from violating this commandment. One of these areas mentioned in the Bible itself is in regard to the toleration of cultic images from alien faiths. We have continual references throughout the Old Testament to the tearing down of the "high places" where this foreign worship was practiced.

A second area in which images may be used sparingly, if at all, is in the native cult, that is, with respect to the worship of God. In some Jewish synagogues are found pictures, but in no sense are these pictures there for the purpose of worship. God provided Moses with a reminder in Deuteronomy 4:15-19, after repeating the second commandment, that he saw no form of God in the fire at Horeb; therefore he should not make unto himself any graven image. This passage in Deuteronomy seems to be underscoring the idea that God is the *Deus Absconditus,* the God who is hidden from our sight, the God who is removed from even our greatest expectations of what He could possibly look like.

Contrast this with the gods of the Egyptians or the Babylonians, with Astarte or Osiris or Lil and Enlil. All of these gods had their visible forms. Were a stranger to come into Egypt and ask to see the god, one could take the visitor into the local temple and show him the image. But to what could the Jew point? The candlestick? The Torah? Clearly, these were not his God. When the Jew was asked, "Show me your god," he repeated Jewish history. He said, "Our God is the one who spoke to Abraham and spoke to Moses; our God is the one who led us out of Egypt." He reiterates these things to himself yearly through the use of the Haggadah and various festivals. The emphasis is upon the hearing of the Word of God that has gone on within his community and the following of that Word.

Perhaps Jesus echoes a very strong sense of the *Deus Absconditus* in John's gospel when He speaks with Nicodemus. "The wind blows where it wishes and you hear the sound of it, but do not know where it comes from and where it is going; so is every one who is born of the Spirit" (Jn 3:8). Jesus seems to suggest that God is as free as the wind, and He moves where He wills. Those who would hear Him are just to listen. Witness as well the Pentecost experience and the emphasis upon the sound of the mighty, rushing wind (Ac 2:1-4). If the emphasis upon the *Deus Absconditus* suggested in Deuteronomy 4 is correct, then perhaps the first commandment stresses the last word and the second emphasizes the first in the Shema: "Hear, O Israel! the Lord is our God, the Lord is one!" (Deu 6:4).

A third area in which the use of images is forbidden by Judaism is with respect to the human image. Because man is created in the image of God, the presence of an image of man in the place of worship is tantamount to having an image of God present. Witness the actions of the Jews in the first century, when Romans such as Gaius attempted to have the Jews worship him. They offered themselves and their families for execution rather than worship Gaius. Were it not for the sympathetic insight of Petronius, Gaius' commander over the Jews, thousands would have died.

In Christian history, quite similar interpretations of this commandment appear. Throughout the book of Acts and in the early church, a tremendous emphasis was placed upon the hearing of the Word of God. In the hearing of the Word of God, faith occurs (Ro 10:17). Using pictures or images for religious purposes in terms of worship is not practiced. Pictures and symbols, however, are found in the catacombs as a reminder of what had gone on in the past. Such historical representations and figures were a means of education, dating from the first to the fourth centuries.

The images referred to in the New Testament which probably come most readily to our minds are the images associated with evil. Somehow the connection between an image and evil seems to still persist. One notable example is found in Revelation, where references are made to the image of the beast who shall come in the end days (chaps. 13, 14, 15, 16, 19, 20).

Yet consider the different use of the word *image* that occurs in Colossians 1:15: "And he [Jesus] is the image of the invisible God." Clearly the term *image* as Paul applies it, has some significant and legitimate usage. This use of *image* does not teach that Jesus is materialistically the Father, but that the very essence of God is involved in the very essence of Jesus. Plato helps us to understand this in the concluding section to the Timaeus, in which he very clearly spells out that the word *icon,* or image, refers to the essence of a given thing. Paul also appears to play on this idea of image in places other than

Colossians. In Romans he writes that the people have "exchanged the glory of the incorruptible God for an image in the form of corruptible man" (Ro 1:23).

An apocryphal story about Abraham in his early days in Ur of the Chaldees speaks of the folly in worshiping graven images. Abraham's father was an imagemaker. On one occasion, after being confronted by God, Abraham went through his father's shop and destroyed all of the images except one very cute little god that sat on a pedestal. In the hands of this god, Abraham placed the hammer he had used to destroy the others. His father was quite enraged at this challenge to his livelihood and demanded to know who had destroyed the gods. Pointing to the little god, Abraham responded, "Ask him, he's got the hammer."

The father said, "But he can't speak."

"That's precisely what I mean to illustrate," Abraham said. "A living god is one who is not formed into images, but can speak, and one whom we must hear."

Anyone wishing to comprehend this commandment should examine each of its component statements in some detail. The first phrase is, "You shall not make for yourself an idol." Earlier translations often render the term *idol* as "graven image," so that the word *graven* (carved) qualifies the kind of image. The word in the Old Testament for image is *peshitta* or *pecel* which refers to a piece of work or a stone chipped away from its natural setting. In other Jewish usage *image* may also refer to inanimate objects. Simon ben Yohai advises that, "A father who does not teach his son the Torah is making him a pecel or an image." In effect such a father is raising a stubborn and refractory son. The idea is this: as an image cut from a rock detracts from the rock as God had made it, even so a person allowed to develop in a way other than that which God intended is becoming a graven image. In the New Testament this idea is stated in, "To one who knows the right thing to do, and does not do it, to him it is sin" (Ja 4:

17). Sin is a distortion of the life as God intended it. Such disfigurement results in a pecel or image.

The commandment goes on to say, "or any likeness of what is in heaven above or on the earth beneath or in the water under the earth." The reference to heaven, earth, and the water under the earth includes reference to the gods of other countries at that time—the sun, the moon, the stars, weather deities, mountains, small worms, sea life, the earth, and the subterranean waters where Osiris is alleged to dwell. The Jew is not to bow down and worship these deities, nor serve them.

In this statement we find a clear reference to the kind of worship associated with the golden calf (Ex 32). Do not be misled in your reading of the golden calf incident. According to the context, we are not to understand that the golden calf was worshiped in the place of God; the calf was worshiped together with God. In this sense, God is jealous. If God seeks you, if He desires your soul to attach to Him, if He keeps you from sin, if He corrects and punishes you, if He becomes indignant and angry, and if He shows any sort of jealousy toward you, see and understand this is for you the hope of salvation.

Paul's famous teacher, Gamaliel, illustrated God's jealousy in answering a critic who asked him the following question: "Heroes are jealous only of other heroes; wise men are jealous of other wise men; rich men are jealous of other rich men; pray tell, of whom is God jealous?"

Gamaliel answered, "Suppose a man were to call a dog, 'Father,' of whom would the father be jealous?"

The critic continued to ask several questions and then finally came to this one, "If these idols serve no useful purpose, then why does not God destroy them?"

Gamaliel responded, "Men worship the sun, the moon, the stars, the mountains, and the hills. Shall God destroy the world for fools?"

Listen and hear the commandment. God is jealous. He desires a pure worship, not a worship which coexists with anything else. The command goes on to say, "Visiting the iniquity of the fathers on the children, on the third and the fourth generations of those who hate Me, but showing lovingkindness to thousands, those who love Me and keep My commandments" (Ex 20:5-6). The phrase "to the third and fourth generations" indicates that God's judgment extends virtually as far as a man can see. The contrast to this is the term "thousands" referring to His infinite mercy, His lovingkindness, and His faithfulness. A comparison of this reference to God's mercy with the statement about His wrath extending to the third and fourth generations shows the phrase does not literally mean "three or four generations" but the entire length of a man's life.

Finally, may we return to Paul. In 1 Corinthians 15:47-49, he writes that men are images, or essences. "The first man is from the earth, earthy; the second man is from heaven. As is the earthy, so also are those who are earthy; and as is the heavenly, so also are those who are heavenly. And just as we have borne the image of the earthy, we shall also bear the image of the heavenly."

If the interpretation of this verse can be drawn out to its fullest extent, we can observe the following with respect to images. God is jealous of any human creation of a form representing Himself, apart from that form which He Himself creates, namely, the essence of Himself that occurs in Jesus. The reason for the prohibition by God of images in the Old Testament is to guard the purity of that one unique image of God that He Himself would one day reveal. The essence of God, the true image of God as opposed to the graven image, is Jesus of Nazareth. Paul goes on to claim that this image of God, which is Christ, is also in Christians. Those who have faith in Jesus are being restored to the essence of their original creation. Christians who are now being renewed in the image of Christ, the image of the second Adam, will in the future fully know this image (Col 3:10). To use John's phrase, "We shall be like Him, because we shall see Him just as He is" (1 Jn 3:2).

The second commandment, then, paraphrased, might read as follows: Make no graven images because, by faith in Jesus, you are already in the image of God. Tremendous implications for personality development are in this commandment. The message seems to be quite clear. In addition to the graven images of stone and wood are graven images of the personality. A man holds to a graven image if he distorts himself from God's plan, if he allows himself to become stubborn and recalcitrant, or if he willfully projects a distorted image of himself for the purpose of feeling better or deceiving others.

The command implies that men are in the image of God. Hence, a psalmist could cry out, "You are precious in the sight of God and even the angels rejoice at your birth." Paul also can advise Christians to respect one another as they are created in God's image. Perhaps the best restatement of the implications of the second commandment comes in the words of Jesus, "Whoever wishes to save his life shall lose it, but whoever loses his life for My sake [that is, he who is remade in my image, the image of God] shall find it" (Mt 16:25).

NOTES

1. G. Campbell Morgan, *The Ten Commandments* (Chicago: Revell, 1901), p. 26.

The Third Commandment

ROBERT E. WEBBER

EXODUS 20:7: *You shall not take the name of the Lord your God in vain.*

When I was asked to speak on this subject, my initial response was one of disappointment. I was disappointed because I really was not persuaded that there was anything in this commandment that you needed to hear. In thinking, meditating, and searching out the meaning of this passage, however, I have completely changed my mind. I have discovered within the positive implication of this commandment something that really speaks to our quest for the reality of God in our lives.

Two words within this text give us insight into its meaning: the word *vain* and the word *name*.

The word *vain* means lacking in reality or truth, empty, or phony. For example, if I damn someone in the name of God, not believing that God will follow through with that damnation, I use His name emptily; I use His name as though He does not exist. Or, for example, if I take an oath in the name of God and really do not think that it matters whether I keep that oath or not, I use His name emptily because I really do not think that He is there to hold me accountable for my words. So what I hear this portion of the text saying is, "Don't try to snow God or anybody else with your empty, useless, trite words about God."

The second word, *name,* refers to the divine character or

personality of God. Thus the third commandment means, "Don't ever attribute divinity or godlikeness to something which is not God, for when you do, you treat the real God as though He does not exist." Whatever we treat as ultimate in our own lives assumes the status of divinity. If man is ultimate in your life, then man is divine. If the process of life is ultimate in your life, then the process of life is divine. If success is ultimate in your life, then success is divine. If material possessions are ultimate in your life, then material possesions are divinity for you. Whatever we treat as ultimate, that is what assumes divinity for us, and then the real God ceases to exist.

So the central, basic, exegetical meaning of the text has to do with our attitude toward God, who lets Himself be known through His name. He had made known the glory of His person through His name (Ex 3:14), and this personal disclosure of Himself was never to be abused by His people. His name is never, under any circumstance, to be used in a wasteful way.

Now let us look at the implications of this text. I am in no way suggesting that these implications derive from the text inherently. Rather they are implications which I have inferred from a twentieth-century context. My suggestion is that the implications of the text are at least twofold. Negatively the text is saying, "Don't ever live as though God does not exist." And positively the text is saying, "Always live in the awareness of God's existence." If that is true, then the third commandment has far-reaching implications. It has to do with my whole life. It has to do with my past, my present, and my future. It has to do with the way I receive, interpret, and grapple with life. It has to do with my perspective, my point of view, my way of seeing things.

The first implication is that we are never to live as though God does not exist. There are obviously many ways we live as though God does not exist, but let me mention just a few.

First, we live as though God does not exist when we make Him into something other than what He is. We live as though He does not exist when we pretend to know exactly who He is, what He is, and what He is doing. We live as though He does not exist when we haughtily assert that He is entirely predictable; under any given set of circumstances we can predict with clarity exactly what He is going to do. As a result we have a magical, commercial, and vending-machine concept of God. We treat Him as though He does not exist when we proudly proclaim that He exists only for us, to run our errands, to make us happy, to pass our tests, to make us successful. We treat Him as though He does not exist when we think of Him as a benign old man, who is sick with loneliness when we do not communicate. We treat Him as though He does not exist when we treat Him like a tribal deity, when we refer to Him in one way or another as an American, as one who is for democracy, as one who is a white Anglo-Saxon Protestant, and, in many cases, as one who is a racist. We treat Him as though He does not exist because we are making Him into something other than what He is.

Second, we treat God as though He does not exist when we think He can be known in a way other than what He can be known. I want to make a special point out of this problem, because I believe many of us are seeking to know God in a way that He is not known; namely through an exclusive emphasis on the mind (rationalism) or an exclusive emphasis on human experience (emotionalism).

How many of us have sought the reality of God through the pursuit of reason? I can remember my whole seminary education as a search for the awareness of God through intellectual means. I sought Him in the text, in systematic theology, in defensive apologetics, and in the study of the history of the Christian church. I was like the knight in Bergman's classic, *The Seventh Seal,* who cried out, "I want knowledge, not faith, not suppositions, but knowledge. I want God to stretch

out His hand toward me, to reveal Himself, and speak to me."
But the sheer intellectual quest for God never satisfied my
deep, interior demand to know that I knew God.

Many of us have also searched for the reality of God
through experience. How many of us have sought to feel God
in our lives? How many of us have heard again and again that
it is normal to experience God? How many of us have walked
the aisle, stood on the mountaintop, or tearfully placed a
faggot on the fire in the hopes of an experience with God—
only to find out again and again that that experience has
fizzled and gone?

My own conclusion is that God is not known through the
mind or through the emotion—but more about that later.

Now let me turn toward the positive implication of this
commandment. You will remember that I suggested that the
positive demand is to live in the awareness of God's existence. But, who is this God before whose existence we must
live? First, let me declare that the God who exists is the *Deus
Absconditas*. He is the God who remains hidden. He is the
God who hides himself from our view. He is the God whose
ways are above our ways, whose thoughts are above our
thoughts. He is the God who is ultimately incomprehensible,
the God who is ultimately unknowable, the God who is ultimately mysterious. He is the God who will not allow Himself
to be boxed in, to be packaged, and to be delivered in a
formula.

Second, this God before whom we are to live is the Lord
of history, the Lord of life. The Hebrews never described
Him in metaphysical terminology. To the Hebrews, God was
never a system or a confession, but the One who acted in history in their behalf. They thought of Him as the Creator,
the Sustainer, the Giver, the Mover of life. They talked of
Him and worshiped Him as the living Lord, the one who
had entered into covenant with their fathers, the one who had
brought them up out of Egypt. And they stood in His pres-

ence, open to the future in full confidence that He who had acted in history for them, was doing His thing in their midst.

But also, this God before whom we are to live is the one who has personalized Himself in Jesus Christ. We know a great deal about God through knowing Jesus Christ. We know that He despises phoniness and externalism. We know that He is angry with people who are so sure that they are always right, with people who elevate forms and rules and regulations. We know that He is angry with people who are insensitive, unkind, unloving, unable to listen, and closed-minded. In Jesus, God is known as the one who responds to real people, like He responded to little children. In Jesus, God is known as the one who is sensitive and compassionate to the needs of the poor and the downtrodden, like He was to the feast-goers, the prostitutes, and the riffraff of society. In Jesus, God is known as the God of wrath who poured out His anger against the sin of the world, on His Son Jesus Christ. But in Jesus, God is also known as the gracious God. Even as Jesus was suffering on the cross for us, He was able to turn to those people who were putting Him to death, and say, "Father forgive them; for they do know not what they are doing" (Lk 23:34). God is known through Jesus as the one who is the victor over what seems to be the final absurdity of life. Three days after they placed Him in the grave, He rose victorious over death, and death, which is our final enemy, lost its sting.

When we are called to live in the awareness of God, we are called to live in the awareness of the God who is ultimately hidden, who is the Lord of life, the Lord of history, and who is personalized in Jesus Christ.

Now, let us turn to the application of our text. If, from the negative point of view, we take God's name in vain by living as though He does not exist, we are met with the immediate demand of knowing this God who exists. If, on the other hand, the positive implication of the text is to live in the awareness of God's existence, we are again confronted with the demand to know God. No matter how you look at this command, it ultimately demands a confrontation between man and God. So the application of the command must answer the ultimate question: how do I become aware of this God whose existence (name) I dare not treat with indifference?

To assume that we can come to know God either through reason or experience is an error. The only way we become aware of the God of the Bible is through proclamation, through announcement, through declaration. In recent days I have come to have a greater appreciation of what the apostle Paul meant when he wrote, "Faith comes from hearing, and hearing comes by the word, [the proclamation, the declaration] of Christ" (Ro 10:17). The word *proclamation* comes from the Greek word *kérussó* which always means "to cry out loud," "to proclaim," "to declare," "to announce." The proclamation of the good news which is in Jesus Christ is not the fancy and persuasive words of the preacher. On the contrary, the proclamation is the act of God through which the thing proclaimed is accomplished. The proclamation is the announcement of the forgiveness of sins in Jesus Christ. When this Word is announced in the Spirit—the forgiveness of sins happens to the one who hears.

Hearing the proclamation is no trick triggered by the swelling of emotional feeling, nor is it a decision prompted by the strength of rational argumentation. An essential feature of Christianity is that it is a religion of the Word—a religion of action, an obedience to the Word. Man does not become righteous as he seeks to apprehend or perceive God by thought or emotion, but as he hears the command of God and observes it. So when we seek the Lord (Jer 29:13), we are not involving ourselves in an intellectual exercise nor an emotional quest, but in a determination to walk in the Word which we have heard and continue to hear.

What does it mean to hear? The word we hear is the word we live by. What do you hear in life? What is of ultimate importance and significance for you in life? If success is of ultimate importance to you, then you hear the word of success. If pleasure is of ultimate significance to you, and if that is the way you live, then you hear the word of pleasure. If popularity is of ultimate importance to you, and that is the way you live, then you hear the word of popularity. But what the apostle Paul is saying and what the third command implies, is that if we hear that Word which is in Jesus Christ—the Word of our acceptance, the Word of our forgiveness, the Word of the new being, the Word of the new humanity—if we hear that Word and live in that Word, then we are in Jesus Christ.

Now, how is all of this related to the third command which demands that we do not treat God matter-of-factly or indifferently? I think many of us are living as though God does not exist because we make Him into the god of our own imagination. We create Him into the kind of god we want Him to be, rather than let Him be what He is. Some of us unknowingly treat Him as though He does not exist because we are seeking to become aware of Him in some other way than simply hearing and living by the proclamation. Some day your little system is going to come tumbling down, and your experience is going to evaporate before your very eyes. If you lose what you consider to be God, and if you lose your way to know God, you will stand in a state of confusion, which will lead to skepticism and ultimate despair.

And now, a word to the skeptics and cynics whose system has come tumbling down and whose experience has dried up. I should like to tell you that you stand in a good position to hear the proclamation of Jesus Christ. Perhaps what disintegrated and evaporated was a figment of your imagination. Perhaps the Spirit of God has taken away your false idols so you can now stand naked before the living God and hear that word of reconciliation that is in Jesus Christ.

This third commandment places us under the wrath of God. The point is that the function of the commandment is to show us that we cannot keep what God declares we must keep. God tells us through the commandment that we must never live as though He does not exist. He tells us that we must always live in the awareness of His reality. When we take that command seriously, we must say to ourselves, "I can't do it." And the more we try, the more we come under condemnation, because we recognize that we cannot keep the standard the commandment demands. So the command shouts out at us that if we live as though God does not exist, and if we live apart from the awareness of the existence of God, we are damned. We are under the wrath of God because we cannot keep the demand of His third command.

But let us not remain in the despair of our inability to keep the third command, for I have good news for you. We stand in a good position to hear the proclamation that we are received, accepted, forgiven, and reconciled in Jesus Christ. The commandment no longer brings the wrath of God nor death. Christ Himself has fulfilled the commandment for us. He has died for our sin, He was raised again for our salvation, and He now brings us forgiveness. In Him we are forgiven. In Him we are reconciled. Now let us live in our forgiveness. Let us live in our reconciliation. Let us live in the hope of the future for we are received in Jesus Christ. We are free! Free to live! Free to be fully human! Live boldly!

The Fourth Commandment

CHARLES HORNE

EXODUS 20:8: *Remember the Sabbath day, to keep it holy.*

The question of the Sabbath is of renewed concern to Christians in our day. With the rapid secularizing of our society, more and more businesses stay open on Sunday. Sports events and entertainment of all types flood into our homes on Sunday by way of television. The question arises whether Christians in large numbers are not being squeezed into this secularized mold. Just how are we to understand the Word of God respecting the Sabbath?

Various theories have been set forth to explain the origin of the Jewish Sabbath. Conservative biblical scholars generally contend that the Sabbath was either Mosaic in origin (Eze 20:11-12) or that it was a creation ordinance (Gen 2:2-3). In any case, the scriptural data makes clear that the major emphasis was upon physical rest. This rest commemorates both what God did for man as Creator (Ex 20:11) and for Israel as Redeemer (Deu 5:15).

In the Mosaic economy in addition to a weekly Sabbath, there was a Sabbath year. This Sabbath year is generally recognized throughout Christendom as ceremonial in character and therefore inapplicable to the church in any literal way. This is not to deny the validity of a moral principle attached to this law which transcends its historically literal interpretation. The Sabbath year taught a permanent truth: God owns all things, and this is to be acknowledged by His creature—man.

The important question in this study is whether the weekly Sabbath has likewise been fulfilled in Christ. Has it also been done away for Christians as an outward institution?

Two major views have been taken toward this commandment. First, some maintain that the setting apart of one day in every seven was a ceremonial, typical, and Levitical custom abrogated with the coming of Christ. This view was held by some of the earliest Christian Fathers (Justin), Roman Catholics, certain of the Reformers and by some present-day Christians. *The Scofield Reference Bible,* for example, has the following note on the Sabbath in connection with Matthew 12:1, "The Sabbath is mentioned [in addition to the gospels] in the Acts only in connection with the Jews, and in the balance of the N.T. but twice (Col 2:16; Heb 4:4). In these passages the seventh-day Sabbath is explained to be, not a day to be observed by the Christian, but a type of the present rest into which the believer will enter when 'he also ceases from his own works' and trusts Christ."[1] Calvin stated that the outward keeping of the Sabbath was abolished together with other figures when Christ came.[2]

Those who maintain this first view believe that the Lord's Day (Sunday) should be observed as a Christian festival for two reasons: (1) because it is a weekly memorial of the victory of the resurrection, and (2) because the example of the church and the enactments of her synods support it. It is observed not because it is now a commandment of God but because of expediency. To sanctify the Lord's Day as a religious rest under the supposed authority of a divine command, is *Judaizing*. Paul states, "Therefore let no one act as your judge in regard to food or drink or in respect to a festival or a new moon or a Sabbath day—things which are a mere shadow of what is to come; but the substance belongs to Christ" (Col 2:16-17). Paul recognizes that strong Christians should regard all days alike (Ro 14:5).

Calvin further states, "There is no doubt that by the Lord

Christ's coming the ceremonial part of this commandment was abolished." But he continues, "Although the Sabbath has been abrogated, there is still occasion for us: (1) to assemble on stated days for the hearing of the Word, the breaking of the mystical bread, and for public prayers (Ac 2:42); (2) to give surcease from labor to servants and workmen."[3]

The Lord's Day (Sunday) was substituted for the Sabbath to show that "the purpose and fulfillment of that true rest, represented by the ancient Sabbath, lies in the Lord's resurrection. . . . Christians are warned not to cling to the shadow."[4]

Second, other Christians hold the view that the Sabbath command is morally binding for all ages, dispensations, and nations. Among groups advocating this position are the conservative Presbyterians, the Dutch Reformed, and those following the Puritan tradition. Robert Dabney, an exponent of this view, states,

> God selected one-seventh as his proper portion of time at the creation, at Sinai, and again at the incoming of the last dispensation. But when the ceremonial law was for a particular, temporary purpose added to the original, patriarchal dispensation, the seventh day became also for a time *a* Levitical holy day and a type. This temporary feature has of course passed away with the Jewish institutions. Upon the resurrection of Christ the original Sabbath obligation was by God fixed upon the first day of the week because this day completed a second work even more glorious and beneficient than the world's creation, by the raising of Christ from the tomb. Hence, from that date to the end of the world the Lord's Day is, by divine and apostolic authority, substantially what the Sabbath day was originally to God's people. It is literally "the Christian Sabbath," and is to be observed with the same sanctity as it was by the patriarchs.[5]

Dabney maintains that according to a creation ordinance, God set apart one day in seven as especially His. Under the Sinaitic covenant, as a matter of temporary ceremonial significance, this seventh day became a Sabbath. With the coming of Christ the temporary ceremonial feature passed away, but the principle of the original creation ordinance now focused on the first day of the week, in commemoration of Christ's resurrection. Thus, from that point in the history of the early church until its end, the Lord's Day (Sunday) is substantially what the Sabbath day was to Israel of old, and it is to be observed with the same seriousness.

The outcome of this position in regard to the practical manner of observing the Christian Sabbath is classically expressed in the *Westminster Confession of Faith*, "This Sabbath is then kept holy unto the Lord, when men, after a due preparing of their hearts, and ordering of their common affairs beforehand, do not only observe an holy rest all the day from their own works, words, and thoughts about their worldly employments and recreations; but also are taken up the whole time in the public and private exercises of his worship, and in the duties of necessity and mercy."[6]

The renowned American preacher and former president of Yale University, Timothy Dwight, in his five-volume work entitled *Theology, Explained and Defended, in a Series of Sermons,* devotes eighty-one pages to an exposition of this view of the Sabbath. In discussing the manner in which it is to be observed, he states in part, "The common and favorite modes of profaning the Sabbath in this way [actions] are spending our time in dress; in ministering to a luxurious appetite; in walking, or riding for amusement; in writing letters of friendship; in visiting; and in reading books, which are not of a religious, but merely of a decent, character; and, ultimately, those which are formed to be the means of amusement and sport."[7]

Having outlined these two views, we may observe that in different ways both positions come to a recognition of the importance of the Lord's Day for rest and corporate worship. In the first position, the Sunday-Sabbath observance is merely spiritually expedient; in the second, the Sunday-Sabbath is obligatory since it is divinely appointed. In the first view, the Sabbath is viewed as a distinctly Mosaic institution with primarily ceremonial significance. Hence, with the passing of that Mosaic age, the Sabbath is not held as obligatory for Christians today. Any moral significance attached to its observance is deemed strictly secondary.[8] In the second position, the Sabbath is viewed as a distinct creation ordinance, antedating the Mosaic law, with primarily moral significance. Hence the Sabbath, though changed to Sunday because of the resurrection of Christ, is held as divinely mandatory for the Christian today. Any ceremonial significance is deemed strictly secondary.

But, we ask, what was Jesus' attitude toward the Sabbath? In examining the New Testament it appears that He did break the Sabbath on a number of occasions by refusing to observe the day according to the Pharisaical tradition (Mk 2:23-24; Lk 13:10-17; Jn 5:9-10). As a devout Jew, He did observe the Sabbath, but He sought to give it its fulfillment that, as a part of the Mosaic economy, it might also be done away with and surpassed by a better order. Jesus sought to teach men that with His coming the Sabbath rest was fulfilled and therefore they would be free from obligation as far as observing the day as such.

An important passage in the theology of the Sabbath is Mark 2:27-28. "And He was saying to them, 'The Sabbath was made for man, and not man for the Sabbath. Consequently, the Son of Man is Lord even of the Sabbath.' " The real question in all the Sabbath disputes in the New Testament was not, Is it right to do good on the Sabbath? But, the issue was this: Is Jesus Lord of the Sabbath?

Christ's followers came to realize that they no longer had an obligation to keep the Sabbath, because they worshiped Him who had fulfilled the Sabbath. In time, because of the resurrection of Christ, the Lord's Day observance arose.

Though the question of the Sabbath is exceedingly complex, I would presently tend to agree with Calvin that the Christian Sunday is not a simple continuation of the Jewish Sabbath "changed into the first day of the week." Instead Sunday rest and worship should be viewed as a distinctly Christian institution adopted after the abrogation of the Jewish Sabbath, as an expedient means of church order and spiritual health and not because of divine obligation.

If this view is accepted, it will set the observance of the Lord's Day (Sunday) in a less legalistic context and free it for a spiritually festive experience. We need not be burdened with what we must not do on this day. Rather, we can rejoice in the liberty which we have in Christ to celebrate what He has done for us. The emphasis is not on the negative note of abuse but on the positive note of celebration.

What then may we say of the central meaning of the Lord's Day? The rest which we take from our ordinary work on this first day of each week ought to remind us that everything which we will and achieve is dependent upon what God has willed and done for us first in Christ. The primary purpose of our Sunday observances is that we should acknowledge God as having the first and last word over all our life. It is an occasion for our placing ourselves in direct relation to the sovereign grace of God and renewing in a special way our submission to His control. It is a time in which we joyously celebrate what Christ has done for us in bringing us into His kingdom.

But even further, we should understand the eschatological significance of our Sunday worship. This is evident from the fact that Sunday is the day of the resurrection of Christ. The early Christians saw in the resurrection of Christ the first clear ray of His final return. They perceived the resurrection as the pledge of an ultimate future redemption and restoration, a guarantee of the revelation of the coming kingdom and eternal life. Hence, the Christian observance of Sunday is not only a matter of resting but primarily of celebration and hope. It is the celebration of a festival. This is the divine service of the community of Christians.

The spiritual rest then which each Sunday celebrates is a rest which is both realized and anticipated. Even now we rest in the finished work of Christ in His death and resurrection for our acceptance before God. We also look forward with expectation for His coming and that day when we shall enter fully into His rest.

What ought Sunday, then, to mean to Christians? Simply this: it is an opportunity afforded to us by sanction of the church to rest from our regular work and to celebrate that spiritual rest which God has provided for His own in Christ— a rest which is both reflective and anticipative. With the psalmist we should be able to say, "I was glad when they said to me, 'Let us go to the house of the Lord' " (Ps 122:1) .

The proper celebration of the Lord's Day requires corporate worship. It is not a private day but one in which the people of God gather for fellowship with God and each other. The manner, time, and place of this worship must be determined in the freedom of the Spirit. "The Lord's Day, above all days, is a day when we have the leisure and opportunity to manifest the collectivity of the Christian faith, to be open to others, to live for one another, to deepen, establish, and cultivate our relationships with all men, and especially those who are of the household of faith."[9]

NOTES

1. *The Scofield Reference* Bible (New York: Oxford U., 1945), pp. 1011-12.
2. John Calvin, *Institutes of the Christian Religion* (Philadelphia: Westminster, 1960), vol. 1, bk. 2, ch. 8, sec. 28, pp. 394-5.
3. Ibid., sec. 32, p. 398.
4. Ibid., sec. 34, pp. 399-400.
5. Robert L. Dabney, *Discussions: Evangelical and Theological* (London: Banner of Truth, 1967), 1:498-499.
6. John Macphearson, *The Confession of Faith* (Edinburgh: T. & T. Clark, 1958), chap. 9, sec. 8, p. 130.
7. Timothy Dwight, *Theology, Explained and Defended, in a Series of Sermons* (New Haven: Dwight, 1836), 3:263.

8. Paul K. Jewett, *The Lord's Day*. Jewett though maintaining that the Sabbath finds its origin in the Mosaic economy nevertheless does not accept this position. It would appear to this writer that it would be easier to argue for Jewett's position on the basis of seeing the Sabbath as a creation ordinance, though he raises interesting, but by no means conclusive, objections to this view.

9. Ibid., p. 167.

The Fifth Commandment

RALPH ALEXANDER

EXODUS 20:12: *Honor your father and your mother, that your days may be prolonged in the land.*

Several years ago following graduation from college, a young girl felt the leading of the Lord to join a particular Christian organization. She took the basic training of this organization and saw the immense need in the world for people to know Jesus Christ. She was thrilled about the prospect of joining the organization, helping to meet the need. However, her parents asked her to live at home for a year and teach school. What should she do? What would you have done? Or perhaps, better still, what was God's desire? I think the Lord speaks explicitly and firmly to this situation, and many others involving parents and children, in the fifth commandment.

The commandment is stated in Deuteronomy 5:16 "Honor your father and your mother, as the Lord your God has commanded you, that your days may be prolonged, and that it may go well with you in the land which the Lord your God gives you." Two issues are raised in this commandment. What does it mean to honor your father and your mother? Second, what does the promise about prolonged life on the earth mean?

Examining those Scriptures which speak of honoring a person, especially parents, we find many interesting concepts enabling us to more fully understand how to honor one's

45

parents. First, to honor is to have reverence and respect for someone with due love. Therefore, when I honor my parents, I lovingly respect and revere them. We likewise read, second, that one who is honored is treated with kindness and is by no means oppressed (Pr 14:31). This should characterize my relationship with my parents. Third, we read that one honors his parents when he is obedient to them and does not go his own way. As Paul writes in Ephesians 6:1-3, "Children, obey your parents in the Lord, for this is right. Honor your father and mother (which is the first commandment with a promise), that it may be well with you, and that you may live long on the earth." Paul makes it very clear within that context that to honor one's parents involves being obedient to them. Fourth, one who honors his parents is not contemptible, quick nor sharp to them nor does he despise them. Exodus 21:15, declares "He who strikes his father or mother with contempt shall be put to death." Or Proverbs 15:5, "A fool rejects his father's discipline. But he who regards reproof is prudent." Fifth, to mock our parents, whether by actions, looks, or words, is not to honor them. Proverbs 30:17 states that the man who mocks his father and mother, shall have his eye plucked out by the ravens and eaten by vultures.

Sixth, to honor one's parents means that he should seek to make them happy. In Proverbs 23:24-25, we read, "A father of the righteous will greatly rejoice, and he who begets a wise son will be glad in him. Let your father and your mother be glad." Finally, we see that honoring one's parents means to provide for their needs, to care for them, especially as they get older. The Pharisees in the New Testament found a way to relieve themselves of this responsibility through a religious, ritualistic vow, in which they pledged to give everything to God. This way they could only use their resources for themselves, until they later gave them totally to the Lord. By this vow they were seeking to get out of ministering to the needs of their parents and of caring for them. Christ spoke explicitly to this situation when he reminded the Pharisees of the fifth commandment. Even when Christ was on the cross He was extremely concerned about the care and needs of his mother.

The Scripture makes it very clear that when one honors his parents it is not to be done in lip service only, but with the totality of the heart. When I honor my parents with all my heart, I respect them, I am kind and helpful, I obey them, I do not treat them with contempt, I do not despise or mock them, but I seek to make them happy and to provide and care for them.

Now concerning the promise, "That your days may be prolonged in the land," two aspects are involved. First, God made a covenant with Abraham in which He made many promises. One promise was that Israel would inherit the land of Canaan. Later God declared that the parents in Israel were to instruct their children in the stipulations of the Mosaic covenant. When the children and the parents were obedient to those stipulations they would live in the land of Canaan, but if they disobeyed the Mosaic covenant they would be taken from the land. Therefore, one aspect of the promise is that the children were to obey the teachings of God taught them by their parents so that they might live in the land and receive the blessings of God throughout life. By way of application to today, if I do not obey the biblical instructions of my parents, I will not appropriate the blessings of those divine truths.

One may immediately say, "Well, what do you do if your parents do not teach you the things of God?" Your disobedience will only compound the problem, for disobedience to parents is never right. The hope of this commandment was that parents would pass on God's truth so that their children, through obedience to the commandments of God as taught by their parents, might be blessed with long life in the land of Canaan.

The second side to this issue is that the parents should communicate to their children what they have learned through their experience, so that their children's lives might be good and prolonged as they obey and follow the advice, instructions, and warnings of their parents. Perhaps this is best summarized in Proverbs 4:10-13 where a father says, "Hear, my son, and accept my sayings, and the years of your life will be many. I have directed you in the way of wisdom; I have led you in upright paths. When you walk, your steps will not be impeded; and if you run, you will not stumble. Take hold of instruction; do not let go." Therefore as that son obeyed the instructions of his father, he would live a good and long life rather than fall prey to the snares of this world. When we follow our parents' advice, we will not find ourselves in situations that are harmful and threatening. As our parents share with us the things of the Lord, and we do them, our lives will be blessed by the Lord, who protects us and prolongs our life.

Speaking of the purposes of this commandment, some of which have been implied already, I see three explicit purposes for the fifth commandment. The first is to teach us authority. In Ephesians 5 and 6 God is comparing Christ's relationship to a believer with that of a husband's relationship to his wife. The husband, by analogy, is in a role like that of Christ, and the wife is in a relationship to him as the believer is to Christ. Therefore, as the child is obedient to the father, he is learning also how to be obedient and respectful to the authority of God. When a child honors and responds correctly to the authority of his parents, it is easier for him to come to know the Lord and to respect and respond properly to His authority. Christ Himself was one who was obedient to the Father and even continued to show obedience in the life which He lived here on earth.

The second purpose of this commandment, as seen in Proverbs 4, is to benefit from our parents' experience so that our life might be productive as we profit from their wisdom. The older I get, the more I respect and realize the value of the many things my parents taught me.

The third purpose of this commandment is to prepare us for life. "Young man, obey your father and your mother. Tie their instruction around your finger so that you won't forget. Take to heart all of their advice. Every day and all night long their counsel will lead you and save you from harm; when you wake up in the morning, let their instructions guide you into the new day. For their advice is a beam of light directed into the dark corners of your mind to warn you of danger and to give you a good life" (Pr 6:20-23, Living Bible). Now regardless of our attitude or the way we respond to our parents—whether we think they are always right or not—God wants us to honor, obey, and respect them, in order that we might learn from each situation, even if it is learning through our irritation when we realize that perhaps they may be wrong. Yet God still wants us to honor, respect, and obey them. God has ordained the family structure in this manner in order that we might properly be trained. He has given you the specific parents that you have to teach you things that only they can teach you. God wants you to learn as you are growing up. If we do not learn then, I am convinced that God will use other people and situations later in life to teach us those things we failed to learn as we grew up. Therefore, this is His sovereign way of instructing us. Through honoring our parents we are prepared for life to live as God meant us to live.

Now I know that there are numerous objections to this commandment. I have had some in the past myself. I would like to look at some of these.

One objection is that this commandment is not valid for today for it is in the Old Testament. In reply to that objection, let me remind you that Christ Himself thought this commandment was important. In fact He told both the Pharisees and the rich young ruler that this commandment was still in effect and still important—just as the other commandments—just as important as not stealing, not committing murder, and so forth. Ephesians 6:1 tells us that the fifth commandment is the right thing to do, and Colossians 3:20 tells us that "this is well pleasing to the Lord." So from God's perspective this is valid and very important. If we wish to please God, we should honor our father and our mother. I am also reminded of the example of our Lord who followed this commandment, for we read in Luke 2:51 that "He went down with them, and came to Nazareth; and He continued in subjection to them [his parents]."

The second objection sometimes raised is "My parents are not Christians; therefore, why should I obey and honor them?" In fact, some say, Ephesians 6:1 reminds us to "obey your parents in the Lord," implying that only Christian parents are to be obeyed. Yet most expositors point out that to be "in the Lord" in Ephesians 6:1 refers to the obeying rather than to the parents. That is, if we are living in the Lord as God meant us to do, we will be obeying our parents. Likewise, Jesus Christ admonished those who had not trusted Him—the Pharisees and the rich young ruler—to observe this commandment. Obedience to this commandment when parents are non-Christians may be the very thing that will lead them to Christ.

This was true in the case of a wife of a friend of mine in seminary. After coming to know Christ, she always felt that as a singer she could only sing Christian songs. Her mother wanted her to sing at teas and parties, and she always refused, feeling it was not godly. Finally her husband had a serious injury, and she had to care for him for several months. Through this she really began to learn what it was to think of others. The next time she had a chance to go home she said, "I'm going to do what my parents want me to do. I want to make them happy. I want to honor them." She stayed out of the kitchen when her mother did not want her there, and she sang when her mother wanted her to.

At the end of her stay her mother said, "What's happened? What's different in your life?" As a result of the daughter's obedience to the fifth commandment, her mother came to know Christ.

Another objection is, "This commandment does not apply to all areas, especially where God has led me differently than my parents." Colossians 3:20 says to obey in all things. Two points need to be remembered. Number one, the Bible makes it very clear that we should not go contrary to the explicit commandments of Scripture. If my parents say to me, "Don't trust Christ," or "Go out and steal and commit murder," then I must not obey them in that point, only because Scripture is very explicit concerning such things. However, at the same time I must place myself in subjection to them for whatever the consequences of my position might be. We must trust the Lord to work in our parents' lives. He is able to do that, and if, perhaps, they have made the wrong decision, God can change their lives. Proverbs 21:1 says, "The king's heart is like channels of water in the hand of the LORD; He turns it wherever He wishes." The same is true with our parents and with our own life.

Some say, "I don't respect my parents, and therefore why should they be in authority over me? They are unfair, they don't understand me. Why should I honor them and be in subjection to them?" We must recognize the difference between the authority and position of our parents in God's chain of command and our attitudes toward our parents (e.g., whether we respect them or whether they understand us). When I was in the ninth grade I can remember a specific substitute teacher. She did not know we had assigned seats. When the bell rang somebody was playing in my seat, so I remained until I could have my chair. The teacher very quickly rebuked me and told me to get into a vacant chair in another part of the room. I did it, rebelling inwardly because I knew that I was right and she was wrong. Because in my heart I dishonored her authority as a teacher, I failed to hear anything else she said in that class.

God wants us to honor our parents even though they may be wrong. They have a position in God's chain of command, in which we are to honor them. We should trust God to work in their lives if they are wrong. The problem is that we do not often want to do that. Some of us say we simply do not want to obey our parents' commands no matter what the rationale might be. That is exactly what the Pharisees said in their tradition, and Christ told them that they were wrong.

A final objection is this: "I am in college and am too old to obey and honor my parents"; or "I am married; therefore I do not need to honor my parents any more." As long as you are single and your parents are providing for you, you still owe obedience to them. If you are married, then the obedience aspect of honoring is no longer operative, because you have established a new home in which the husband is now the head. However, all other aspects of honoring still apply for the rest of your life. Listen to their advice. Provide and care for their needs.

What do we do now? Let me make a brief suggestion. I suggest that you submit yourself in honor to your parents in the power of the Spirit of God. For Ephesians 6, in its context, shows that this is what is done as one is living in the power of the Spirit. I suggest also that you expect, by faith, the omnipotent God to work in the lives of your parents as well as your own. He can do exceeding abundantly above all that you ask or think (Eph 3:20). Things impossible with men are possible with God (Lk 18:27). I also suggest that you ask their forgiveness for those areas where you have failed to honor them—not with the condition that they have to admit that they have been wrong or with the condition that you expect them to change. But out of honor for them, ask that they forgive you if you have failed to honor them in any way.

Finally, if your parents should ask you to do something explicitly contrary to the Word of God, submit creative alternatives as Daniel did when the king asked him to do something contrary to the Word of God. Daniel did not argue, but in a spirit of grace, submitted an alternative. I suggest that you sit down and talk with your parents in this way and submit an alternative in Christ.

The girl that I mentioned in the beginning went home in obedience to her parents and taught school for a year. Today she will tell you how thankful she is that she did—for at the conclusion of her year at home, her parents were killed in an automobile accident. What if she had not obeyed God and His Word? God's way is perfect, and His way is to honor our father and our mother.

The Sixth Commandment

Arthur F. Holmes

EXODUS 20:13: *Thou shalt not kill* (KJV).

With this commandment we enter the second table of the law. The whole law is summed up in the command to love the Lord our God and to love our neighbors as ourselves (Mt 22:37-39). It has been suggested that while the first table of the law directly addresses our love for God, the second extends love to our fellowman. Love is not just personalized concern devoid of specific moral obligations, as the so-called new morality affirms. Love is an active concern for every aspect of a person's well-being, and so the second table of the law spells out unchanging moral obligations which love must accept in regard to life and death, to sex and marriage, to property rights, to truth and reputation, and to attitudes toward other people.

Obviously the law cannot make people love one another. But it can, to a considerable extent, ensure the just treatment which love desires. The second table of the law, therefore, has social as well as individual application. It provides the basis for a social ethic and lays the groundwork for civil legislation that will further social justice. The nation of Israel was to be a just society, because its laws rested on the moral law of God.

Let us label the purpose of the law, and of the sixth commandment in particular, "moral persuasion." It is one of the means God uses to guide our lives and to order society. The law cultivates in us a moral conviction about violence, about practicing love and justice here on earth, and about our personal, social, and political responsibilities.

Legalism is very different from the true purpose of law. It appears in at least three guises. First, legalism thinks of justice not in terms of love but in terms of fear. It is afraid of retribution for sin and failure. It stresses retributive justice rather than the distributive justice that is concerned for other people. But the grace of God, which delivers us from that kind of fear, delivers us also from that kind of legalism (Ps 32; Ro 8:1-4). Second, legalism hopes to escape retribution by obeying the law perfectly. It has not fully accepted the depth of human sin, nor learned that the law of God draws men to dependence on God's grace (Gal 3:21-24). Third, legalism builds a wall against human error by developing laws for every situation that might arise and claiming for these laws universal and unchanging validity. It leaves no room for the painful moral decisions with which all of us are confronted in ambiguous or novel situations. Legalism has all the answers and tolerates no disagreement. It fails to see that in a tangled and twisted world, we are often left to choose between alternatives, all of which involve evil, and some of which are so complex that agreement—even among Christians—is virtually impossible and human error is almost inevitable. A man must act with faith in God's mercy.

We need to recognize that the Bible itself contains two kinds of rules. Some, like the second table of the law, are unchanging, universal moral obligations stated in general terms. Others, as in Exodus 21-23, apply those moral obligations to changeable particular situations. The first kind we may call "moral laws," the second "prudential rules." The legalist elevates all rules to the level of moral laws, while the new morality reduces them all to prudential rules. As we shall see more fully, the two are distinguishable in Scripture and must be distinguished in our thinking.

"Thou shalt not kill" (Ex 20:13, KJV). We have considered the purpose of this commandment and of moral law in general. But what about the meaning of the sixth commandment itself? The Hebrew verb has no special technical sense, as if a certain kind of killing is intended. As a result several possible interpretations arise. In order to decide between them we must examine the scope of moral obligation for human life, as this comes out in the social legislation of the Old Testament; a complete study should include the preaching of the prophets and the ethical teaching of all Scripture.

Some have taken the sixth commandment to forbid all killing, at least the taking of human life. This last qualification is important, for Scripture does not hallow other forms of life, as is sometimes the case in Eastern religions. When God warned Noah about taking human life, it was because man is made *in the image of God* (Gen 9:6). But granted that it is human life with which we are concerned, does the commandment forbid *all* taking of human life under any circumstances whatever?

I think not. In the Old Testament, at least three kinds of killing are explicitly delineated from murder. One is accidental manslaughter, in which case offenders could escape vengeful blood feuds by taking refuge in certain cities designated for this purpose (Ex 21:12-14; Num 35:10-34; Deu 19:4-13). Another is killing in self-defense (Ex 22:2-3), although Jesus' advice to turn the other cheek has occasionally been taken to mean that Christians are expected to let themselves be killed rather than kill. Another is capital punishment, which in the Old Testament was permissible not only for murder and patricide (Ex 21:14-15), but also for kidnapping (Ex 21:16), for witchcraft (Ex 22:18), for idolatry (Deu 13; 17:2-8), for sexual intercourse with animals (Ex 22:19), for adultery (Lev 20:10), for incest (Lev 20:11-12), for homosexual acts (Lev 20:13-15), and for radical contempt of court (Deu 17:8-13). Capital punishment was permissible in all these cases but not mandatory, for it was not enforced in the case of David's adultery with Bathsheba or Jesus' treatment of the woman taken in adultery (Jn 8:1-11). I shall have more to say on this subject in a moment, but my point now is that capital punishment is not murder, nor is accidental manslaughter, nor is killing in self-defense. The commandment, then, does not treat all killing the same, without regard to different kinds of killing and different situations.

Some interpreters therefore confine the prohibition to deliberate murder. I am not satisfied with this, for while accidental manslaughter is not as blameworthy as murder, the offender is still made to suffer for his mistake. Criminal negligence is still a culpable offence. Moreover, the Bible protects the life and safety even of slaves and unborn infants, and requires compensation for physical injuries received either in a fight or from an animal someone else owns (Ex 21:18-32). Physical punishment must be administered with care so as to avoid needless injury and risk to life (Deu 25:1-3), and explicit warnings are given about self-inflicted injury (Deu 14:1-2) and gang violence (Ps 94:1-11; Pr 1:10-19). It seems that more than murder is in mind in the sixth commandment.

Consequently I prefer a third interpretation. We are to guard against *all* kinds of needless violence and criminal negligence. As Keil and Delitzsch put it, "Not only is the accomplished fact of murder condemned, whether it proceed from open violence or stratagem ([Ex] xxi:12, 14, 18), but every act that endangers human life, whether it arise from carelessness (Deut. xxii:8) or wantonness (Lev. xix:14), or from hatred, anger, and revenge (Lev. xix. 17, 18)."[1] Stated positively, it means we must value human life because God made man in his own image.

How does the commandment, interpreted in this fashion, apply to our own day?

Take the problem of highway safety and gun control legislation. The question we must ask, it seems to me, is this:

what can morally responsible people do, in love and justice, about the threat of uncontrolled carelessness to human life and safety? The sixth commandment suggests I should be cautious about driving and the use of lethal weapons, and that I support responsible legislation and good law enforcement on such matters.

Take the problem of abortion and euthanasia. The question we must ask here is this: under what circumstances, if any, may morally responsible people decide the life or death of another human being? It is a complex question, for in order to answer it, we must also decide when a human being becomes human and when he ceases to be such. But do not give the glib response: never under any circumstances may one person decide another's life or death. For then what will you say about our next case?

Take capital punishment. In view of the biblical precedents we cannot say it is essentially and always immoral. In biblical times, it was an accepted and justifiable means of law enforcement and criminal punishment. In view of the intrinsic value of human life and regardless of what a person has done, are other methods now available which are at least as effective in deterring the criminal and protecting society, methods which may also enable the criminal to become a contributor to society rather than a threat? Are there effective alternatives? This, I take it, is a prudential question that calls for sociological input, not a political question alone and not a simple question about the moral law.

Finally, take the agonizing topic of war. Here I suggest essentially the same question applies as in the case of capital punishment: in view of the intrinsic value of human life of both friend and foe, are other methods now available for deterring the aggressor and securing peace and justice, methods which may also enable the conflicting parties, whatever their differences, to work together in some ways for the common good? Our moral responsibility here is first for the prevention and avoidance of war, for exploring every alternative available, and creating new alternatives to war. We are also responsible for limiting the extent of war, for limiting its intensity, for preventing atrocities, and punishing those who commit them. Likewise we are responsible for ameliorating the consequences of war on friend and foe alike. In this every Christian and every morally responsible person should agree, whatever our other differences on the subject.

The biblical attitude to war is mixed. On the one hand war is regarded as evil; bloodshed and violence are lamented, the psalmist glories in a God who makes wars to cease and destroys the weapons of war, and the prophets look for one who shall bring peace and justice to earth. On the other hand, war is recognized realistically as a tragic fact of life: God allows and even uses war in accomplishing His own just purposes; He strengthens our hands and gives us the wisdom we need for success in war.

The tension between the tragedy of war and the hope of peace has persisted throughout Christian history. On the one hand, the pacifist rejects war in any form even in self-defense and reverts either to nonresistance or to passive resistance. On the other hand, the just war tradition works for limitations on war through moral persuasion and a structure of international law. Both are Christian traditions; both regard war as an evil to be outlawed; and both seek peace—the one by refusing military service, and the other by placing moral limitations both on entry into war and on the extent and means of conflict.

Three considerations seem central in the Christian's relationship to war.

(1) The sixth commandment is not addressed to the problem of war. It forbids murder and other needless killing without ruling out the killing that may become a tragic necessity for a society in upholding peace and justice. The law is intended to provide moral restraints on violence, to teach the

sanctity both of human life and of social order, and to prevent a private individual both from taking life and from taking the law into his own hands.

(2) The New Testament ethic of love summarizes the content and expresses the spirit of the Old Testament law. We are told to love our enemies, to practice mercy rather than retaliation, and, if at all possible, to live peaceably with all men (Mt 5:38-48; Ro 12:18-21) . Christian pacifists base their position here, claiming that the law of love rules out violence and war under any circumstances and that the Christian is bound to a higher law than that of the state. The just war theory stresses the agreement of the New Testament ethic with Old Testament teaching. But while it allows that force may sometimes be necessary, it insists that the law of love must infuse and transform society's enforcement of peace and justice. Both views, in other words, insist on applying the law of love to war.

The new morality confuses the issue by claiming that love is the only moral principle, and by defining love as personal relationship. This is an existentialist view, not a biblical view of love. In the New Testament, love is indeed personal, but the law of love is also said to summarize other moral laws, not to supersede them. Two fundamental moral principles appear in both the Old and the New Testament, as they do in philosophical ethics: love and justice. Love is the spirit and summation of the law; justice is the structure and operation of law that secures peace and human rights. Love and justice are equally concerned with people, and equally basic. The biblical ethic derives from the character of God, who is both loving and just.

(3) The pursuit of justice in society requires both legislation and the enforcement of law. Civil law is morally binding on the citizen because of the contractual basis of our democratic institutions, but it is also morally binding because government is part of God's order for His creation (Ro 13:1-7) .

Most Christians, therefore, agree that limited force may be needed to restrain lawbreakers. But they do not agree on the application of this principle to those who violate peace and justice between nations.

The Christian pacifist claims that nonviolence serves peace and justice more effectively than does war, and thereby he bears witness to a higher law than that of the nations. He believes that his citizenship in the kingdom of God takes priority over political responsibilities and military service. The just war tradition, on the other hand, appeals to the Old Testament prophets. It insists that war is an evil, but it claims that limited and defensive war may sometimes reduce the evil in a torn and unjust world. War may then become the least of several evils, and in that case the Christian may fight. At the same time, however, he must bring love and justice to the conflict, not only by his conduct in military service, but also by political activity, through prayer and preaching, and every legitimate influence. The just war theory, in other words, does not attempt to justify war. It attempts to limit the evils of war as much as is posible in a fallen world by moral persuasion and by international law. It allows war as a last resort in self-defense, but never for economic or political gain. It insists on limited weaponry and condemns the use of needless force and pointless violence.

Clearly the application of the sixth commandment is complex and controversial. In regard to medical ethics, to capital punishment, and to war, disagreement and unresolved problems remain because this is not an ideal world, and we cannot see or act as we ideally should. The perfect option no longer exists; man is fallen. Whatever we do will be second best. It is a tragedy that anyone needs to be a pacifist, or to develop a just war theory, or to consider euthanasia, or to vote for or against capital punishment. But we are still morally responsible to ask the right questions, to seek justice, and to practice love as best we can.

What can we do to implement the sixth commandment more fully in our day? My suggestion is this. If we are to apply the sixth commandment to our society, we must learn to use moral persuasion as it was used in Old Testament days through prophetic preaching, through legislation, and other means. Therefore, we need morally informed, morally responsible people at strategic points in society. We need them in international affairs, in national and local government, in criminology, in law enforcement and the military, in medicine and medical ethics, in the mass media, and in education. We need Christian preachers with the courage and the wisdom of the Old Testament prophets who will apply the law of God to the life of our land. The commandment, then, becomes God's call to bring love and justice to bear in the conflicts and violence of a broken world, in eloquent testimony to the redeeming love and the justice of God Himself.

NOTES

1. J. F. Keil and F. Delitzsch, *Biblical Commentary on the Old Testament,* vol. 2, "The Pentateuch" (Grand Rapids: Eerdmans, 1949), p. 123.

The Seventh Commandment

MORRIS INCH

EXODUS 20:14: *You shall not commit adultery.*

In the 1631 edition of the King James Version of the Bible, the printers omitted the word *not* from the seventh commandment. For those who secured a copy of the Scriptures, the text read: "Thou shalt commit adultery." Thereafter this particular edition was known as the "wicked Bible," and the king's printers were fined for their lapse. We are no doubt wise to consider the text which prohibits adultery rather than this notable exception.

At the outset, the commandment seems to be a very straightforward statement, relatively unambiguous, but there are aspects and implications which are rather subtle. Adultery, by its strictest definition, refers to having sexual intercourse with a woman who is betrothed or married to another. In a broader sense it comes to mean any violation of the sanctity of sex. In this latter connection, the rabbinic commentary sets forth gradations of gravity in the offense, depending on whether the other partner involved is unmarried, in her menstrual period, married, a heathen, another male, or a beast.

A helpful generalization, but not a strictly accurate statement, is the observation that with Jesus' teaching on adultery the emphasis was shifted from *act* to *attitude*. The commandments were not unconcerned with attitude as seen in the injunction against coveting. Neither is Jesus unconcerned with the act as evidenced in the way He dealt with the adulterous

woman, to whom He said: "Go . . . sin no more" (Jn 8:11).
He did not tell her to continue, but watch her attitude.

In the Sermon on the Mount, Jesus did not decrease the objection to adultery, but pointed to the lust from which it
springs and to certain implications of the commandment for
marriage (Mt 5:27-32). Jesus stressed the need for a life of
purity, a moral integrity which goes beneath the act, through
the overtures which lead up to it, and to the imaginations
which conceived it. Harvey Cox, in his widely read *Secular
City*, tells of a recent college graduate who prided herself in
keeping her virginity intact while regularly petting to orgasm.
By some peculiar mental gymnastics, she was able to extract
the act from the larger context of meaningful life in which
Jesus spoke of sex and its abuse.

"Every one who looks on a woman to lust for her has committed adultery with her already in his heart" Jesus concludes
in Matthew 5:28. One does not solve the problem by stopping
short of intercourse while feeding the desire within. A more
radical surgery is necessary: if your eye offend you, pluck it
out, and if your right hand offend, cast it off. That is to say,
remove anything from your life which causes you to sin. But
what is Jesus asking us to reject? Is it sex relationships or the
aspiration for such? Hardly either. Not a healthy interest in
sex, but adulterous lust is the object of the Lord's scathing
rebuke.

The Master next turns to an application of moral purity
in the case of marriage. The spirit of His words have been
accurately captured in the marriage ceremony: "till death do
us part." There is none of the "let us leave the back door
open in case things do not go well." Certainly a high degree
of risk is involved in such a life commitment, but the most
worthwhile things in life require a commensurate risk.

Granted the ideal and even given the best intentions, some
marriages still end in shipwreck. Moses recognized this fact.
He was a realist. "Whoever divorces his wife, let him give her

a certificate of dismissal," he conceded. The certificate of divorce was necessary to clarify the woman's status, and was the means of delivering her from the whims of her husband. And while the woman in that culture was not permitted to divorce her husband, she could appeal to the courts and compel him to divorce her under certain circumstances. The whole subject of divorce was a critical one; the school of Shammai took a stricter interpretation which allowed only unchastity and perhaps immodesty as legitimate causes for initiating proceedings, while the school of Hillel allowed virtually anything short of frivolous reasons. While the Lord's answer, on the surface at least, seems to expose the sterner school of interpretation, He actually transcends the argument by stressing the matter of inner rectitude. The phrase: "and whoever marries a divorced woman commits adultery" (Mt 5:32) is aimed primarily at the callous husband who disregards the sanctity of his marriage.

To the early church was bequeathed both the teaching and the task of legislating hard cases. For instance, Paul indicated that the Christian's respect for marriage should not be used as an excuse for hindering a disbelieving partner from leaving, or the norm of a Christian union to be the rationale for dissolving a mixed marriage (1 Co 7:12-16). The apostle's instruction reflects the concern of the Master for the welfare of the wife and children who are involved.

Jesus' emphasis on life's sanctity is everywhere evident in the teaching of the early church, such as in the *Didache* where adultery is listed under the "Way of Death" and opposed to the "Way of Life." The *Didache* further places adultery in juxtaposition to loving God and our neighbor, as a breakdown in relationships: divine and human.

Whereas the *Didache* sees the commandment as a guide to life, Joseph Fletcher, in his best seller *Situation Ethics,* seems to transfer it over to the death side of the ledger. You may recall that Fletcher has a section which he entitles "Sacrificial

Adultery," followed by an account which I will summarize briefly.

During the closing days of the World War II, a German mother of three children had left her youngsters to secure food, only to be apprehended and imprisoned by Russian soldiers. A short time after this her husband was released from a prisoner-of-war camp, managed to locate the children, and tried to reestablish the home as best he could while trying to find out what had become of his missing wife. Eventually word of her husband's struggle came to the woman in her imprisonment. Wanting to be of help to her loved ones, she began to muse over the options open to her. One was to become ill, in which case she would be removed to a hospital for treatment and convalescence and eventually returned to the prison camp. So this would not do. The other possibility was to become pregnant, and in this case outright release could be expected. Thinking it over, weighing the pros and cons of the situation, she finally decided to take this latter direction and approached a guard to accommodate her. Pregnancy resulted, and the woman was dismissed from the prison compound to rejoin her family.

As Fletcher describes the reunion, it was joyful and undiminished by the circumstances which brought it about. When subsequently the child was born, he was not only accepted but especially loved because of the sacrifice he represented.

The effect of Fletcher's storytelling wizardry is to pit law (the commandment against adultery) against love and life, which seems in violation of the clear teaching of Scripture and the subsequent experience of the church.

Fletcher stops at the point where everything is going along very nicely, but I would like to introduce an apocryphal account of what happened thereafter.

Several weeks after the child was born the foster father was in the local beer parlor with one of his cronies of many years standing. The fellow looked at him with that sort of knowing and unnerving expression that people can get on their faces, and said, "My, that really was a story your wife told you, wasn't it?"

The husband was offended and threatened to punch his friend in the nose.

Surprised, the other explained, "Oh, I'm sorry. I didn't mean to anger you. You know we have been good friends for many years. I thought this was a story given out for public consumption. I didn't realize that you took it seriously."

Now the husband put the insinuation out of his mind; so he did the next day, and the day after that. But eventually he found himself sitting home at night looking at the infant and wondering. The wife soon realized something was wrong, but the husband did not feel free to discuss his suspicion, and things went from bad to worse. We need not dwell on the festering problem further, but notice how what seemed such a probable solution previously now began to take on negative considerations. Perhaps, if the woman had waited just a little longer, the transition from war to peace would have allowed her release, and none of this alienation would have occurred.

Let us take the story one step further. We tend to overlook the guard, whose cooperation was solicited, and reduce him to a mere instrument. How insensitive! People are more than things to be used. Unfortunately, in this case the man's involvement had an exceedingly bad aftereffect. He decided to extend his service to other female prisoners, even when they did not solicit his attention, and because of his indiscretion gained the wrath of his superiors. Recently we heard that this man died in Siberia after being banished there for the trouble he had caused.

As admitted at the beginning, this is an apocryphal episode. (The original story may also be fanciful.) The point is that one cannot reason backward; he must not take the exceptional development to prove the rule for decision-making. In contrasting love and life with law, Fletcher leaves us with a mistaken picture of life itself.

Consider next a biblical illustration from Genesis 26. Rebecca and Isaac went to live among the Philistines. Isaac recognized that Rebecca was a very lovely woman, and that it was not uncommon for a husband to lose his life to those who shared his appreciation for the attractiveness of his spouse. The patriarch decided that discretion was the better part of valor and pretended that Rebecca was his sister. This pretense carried along for a time until one day Isaac was making some very unsisterly approaches to Rebecca, and the Philistinian magistrate, Abimelek, observed his deportment. The king called Isaac in and in effect said to him, "Isaac, I'm not stupid; I see what is going on and what you are building up to, and I recognize that this is something meant to take place in the bonds of marriage. Why have you deceived us? Someone might have unsuspectingly violated your marriage bond and brought down divine judgment upon us." Abimelek understood what the patriarch in his fear had conveniently overlooked—the benefit of law in structuring life and fostering love.

The preferable alternative to Fletcher's analysis is, as I see it, that law and love are life complements rather than in opposition to each other. This conclusion is the impact of the illustration and the impress of the commandment.

Finally, something of my own experience. I love my wife. I am not saying this for her benefit. Other occasions are more appropriate for telling her this. But I affirm my love as a preface to what follows.

There are times when I feel more drawn to my wife than on other occasions. Without the commandment we might be unduly tempted to turn away from each other, perhaps to someone else. But the fact that we are married, that we have exchanged vows and are observing these vows, has been the means of reminding us of our relationship. Our affection springs back to conscious awareness and excites us with the possibilities of sharing together. On the other hand, when I need no reminder, when I am keenly aware of the bond, love becomes sort of a celebration of the law, and I say to myself, "How good and wise God is, and how merciful in His establishment of the marriage covenant!"

Then, the children must be considered. How difficult it is for youngsters to experience parents playing the game of partner exchange, and sometimes even worse, the incredible hostility that develops when only the formal recognition of marriage has survived. God means something better for these little ones. Jesus said it is better that a millstone weigh us down to a watery grave than we offend them (Mt 18:6). How much better to swallow one's pride and get on with making a home where children will be raised in the "Way of Life"!

Thinking of law and love as complementary aspects of living and seeing in the seventh commandment God's compassionate wisdom, I cannot help but say, "God is good!" Certainly He does not withhold anything that is for my benefit. Thanks be to God for the abundant life.

When we have taken this perspective on life, some difficult decisions still confront us. But the way to work through these problems is not by perverting the divine perspective. By doing so, we become the larger problem. Let us see life as a whole and get an integrated view of living. We must seek God's will and find the way where we cease to be the obstacle and become part of God's solution.

The Eighth Commandment

DONALD HAGNER

EXODUS 20:15: *You shall not steal.*

> So it came about on the third day, when it was morning, that there were thunder and lightning flashes and a thick cloud upon the mountain and a very loud trumpet sound, so that all the people who were in the camp trembled. . . . Mount Sinai was all in smoke because the Lord descended upon it in fire; and its smoke ascended like the smoke of a furnace, and the whole mountain quaked violently (Ex 19:16-18).

Well might the mount have quaked, and the people have trembled on this occasion. The infinite, omnipotent God, sovereign Creator, and Lord of the universe deigns to speak to fallen mankind. What creature will not tremble at the prospect? The commandments thunder forth from Sinai, and the very absoluteness of the "Thou shalts" and the "Thou shalt nots" makes the blood run cold. The inexpressible awesomeness of God Himself, of which the visible manifestations at Sinai are but a token, is enough to bring a paralyzing fear upon the man who hears these words.

There is this aspect to the Sinai revelation, and we Evangelicals would do well to recapture some of this awe for the Almighty God. But there is another aspect to Sinai which we ought not to forget. Fearsome though this event is, the God of Sinai has already chosen, in love, and entered into a covenant with the people to whom He speaks. The commandment grows out of the covenant, and for this reason the Jew rightly treasures the law as his most precious possession. But since the law presupposes the covenant, it should not be seen in isolation from the covenant. We ought not to think of the Ten Commandments as the arbitrary dictates of a remote God which He forces on us for no other reason than to make us subject to His will. They are, rather, an expression of His own character as manifested in covenant love.

If we can see the commandments as expressions of the essential character of God, they will no longer appear unrelated to the grace that has come to us in Jesus Christ. The very fact that Jesus can summarize the commandments in one word *love* demonstrates that they are an expression of God's character, for "God is love" (1 Jn 4:8), and Jesus Christ is the gift of that love. It follows that the commandments are intrinsically related to the very essence of Christianity. And that is true of the eighth commandment, "You shall not steal," (Ex 20:15).

First, I want to look at the nature of stealing seen theologically. To steal is to go directly counter to the very heart of Christianity. Preeminently our faith has to do with giving. God has given to us in the past, continues giving to us in the present, and will give to us in the future. This is the meaning and miracle of grace: God freely gives to the undeserving. For this very reason, the Christian who is being conformed to the image of his Lord is characterized by the fact that he gives. He is no longer obsessed with his own affairs, his own possessions, his own life. The center of gravity in his life has shifted from self to Christ, and he now lives to be of service to God and man. He that has known grace must in turn show grace.

Diametrically opposed to the Christian attitude, however, is that of the nonchristian world. While for the Christian, life consists in giving, for the non-Christian, life consists in getting. Our society in particular is dominated by an insatiable lust for acquisition. From virtually every direction—from the TV, the radio, the magazines and newspapers, the billboards, the flashing neon lights, and from the endless string of shops, stores, and discount markets—we are incessantly bombarded with the credo of American society: to get is to live. We have rewritten the Scripture to read, "Truly, truly a man's life *does* consist in the abundance of his possessions."

Of course biblical theology sees nothing wrong with a man acquiring things or possessing and enjoying them—as long as his life is not dominated by them. Indeed, the eighth commandment guarantees the right of personal property. Christianity does not negate the world in this sense. It affirms the world, for God "supplies us with all things to enjoy," (1 Ti 6:17). Stealing, however, simultaneously contradicts the essence of Christianity and gives allegiance to the materialism of a sick society. The person who steals says in effect, "It is I who am of ultimate importance and nothing shall stand in the way of my self-gratification. I live so that I might get for myself." Stealing is rooted in egocentrism and is thus related to other matters covered by the commandments. Thus lying and stealing often occur together; indeed, lying is often a form of stealing and stealing a form of lying. Similarly, covetousness is most often the sin that precedes and gives birth to actual deeds of theft. Stealing also involves a violation of the first commandment, for it involves an ego idolatry at the expense of the lordship of God.

Let us look a little more closely at what constitutes stealing. The basic definition is, of course, to take that which is not rightfully one's own. There are, to be sure, a large number of different ways in which this can be done. Overt thievery is the most obvious one. This has always been a problem in human society, but where life is seen to consist in the abundance of material things a man possesses, the problem is compounded. In our society robbery continues to increase alarmingly. Shoplifting has grown to enormous proportions. Libraries suffer the loss of thousands of dollars worth of books annually. Overt theft. Yes, we know the problem. But surely we are above that here on our campus. One would hope so, but one only needs to speak to the people in the bookstore, the library, the business office, and in the dorms to find out otherwise. There are some of us who need to confess and make restitution. God give us the strength to do so.

While most of us would find it difficult to steal from another person, we find it relatively easy to steal from an impersonal organization. We rationalize that we are underpaid and overworked. We are not fairly treated. The heads of the organization grow fat at our expense. What little one may filch in whatever way from such a corporation, establishment, or organization will not be missed. It is the little man against the establishment; surely the little man is justified in an occasional dip into the till. Petty thievery of this sort is almost a way of life in our world. It is a part of the overall web of graft, extortion, embezzlement, bribery, confidence rackets, and crime syndicates, that has spun itself over our society. Everybody is out to get the almighty dollar.

Of course, very often it is not only the employee who is guilty of stealing but also the employer. The producer of consumer goods steals in a rather different way. With all the good that capitalism entails, it must be admitted that the capitalistic obsession with profit making has meant evil for our society. Profit making constitutes the cult of the American credo: to get is to live. The producer insidiously infects our minds with advertising calculated to deceive, advertising which panders to blatant hedonism and neurotic self-gratification, advertising which gives voice to the philosophy of the day as typified by the commercial which argues that you only come this way once, so you'd better get as much out of life as you can. The shiny exterior of the new product you buy is more often than not hiding shoddy workmanship of an article that will soon fall apart, but which will have accomplished its main purpose—not service but profit making. Now, I am in favor of free enterprise and profit making. But where it is not conditioned by responsibility, conscientiousness, and the genuine desire to serve the consumer, it degenerates into a form of stealing. Capitalism, with its greed for gain untempered by the Christian ethic, has permeated our society both economically and psychologically. Unconsciously we have become enslaved to the profit principle in many other areas beside commerce.

Most of us, however, are quite sophisticated and subtle in our violation of the eighth commandment. We would not openly take something that did not belong to us or which we did not purchase. Nor would we pawn off on another an object of less than its apparent worth. But we do allow more subtle forms of thievery which are no less violations of the commandment. We see our way clear for just a little cheating here and there, a little craftiness, some careful plagiarism, a few white lies, a little juggling of the figures, a little fudging on the tax return, a little more pay than we deserve, a little higher price than the product warrants, et cetera, ad nauseam.

We are comforted in these minor infringements by society-at-large which finds them not only quite acceptable, but even praiseworthy in some respects. "After all," comes the final justification, "everybody does it." Indeed, so hardened do we become to these dishonesties that they become second nature to us. Diogenes, the cynic philosopher of ancient Greece, was nobody's fool when, during the daylight hours, he carried about a lantern in search of an honest man.

Stealing, then, consists not only of overt acts of theft, but also of any dishonesty calculated to bring gain in any form to one's own person. Precisely because so much of our society is shaped and motivated by the idea of self-gain, the Christian is called to swim against the current. He is called to be scrupulously honest and just in the affairs of his life. More than that, he is called to share, to give, and to help. I suggest that one of the most difficult tasks facing the church in America today is that of defining the role and establishing the identity of the Christian vis-a-vis a society ruled by materialism and a world trapped in poverty.

Ordinarily we think of stealing as involving only man— that is, man stealing from man. This is certainly its primary meaning in the Old Testament context. We have taken a quick glance at the great variety of ways that man steals from man. But when looked at theologically, may it not be that the commandment has a broader application? Is it not possible for man to steal from God?

There is some New Testament warrant for answering yes to this question. Jesus Himself referred to false prophets as thieves and robbers. (Jn 10) who try to plunder the sheep from the shepherd. The person who attempts to find acceptance with God apart from Jesus Christ, the door of the sheepfold, is guilty of attempted theft. That is, he has tried to gain for himself that which can in no way be regarded as rightfully his.

We see again the interrelatedness of the commandments, the nature of God, and the nature of man. We are at the root of man's basic sin—his egocentricity, his self-centeredness. The sin of Adam, bringing ruin upon his progeny, was motivated by the desire to gain that which was not rightfully his—to be like God. Satan lured Adam and Eve into attempted theft. Unbiblical attempts to achieve acceptance with God all violate the commandment—"You shall not steal." And the joyful paradox that comprises the heart of Christianity is that what man cannot steal, God has given freely.

But I would suggest that there are other ways that we can steal from God. To misuse the gifts that God showers upon us is a form of robbery. Make no mistake about it. To squander time and ability is to steal from God. I do not mean to suggest that the use of time or the development and application of talents in any area other than what is traditionally called Christian service is illegitimate. What I speak of does not involve the false dichotomy between sacred and secular; it involves the careful determination of what is the improper use of God's gifts for me, whether within or outside of Christian service. All of us are called to a balanced life wherein we become fully developed and whole persons who can enjoy the world that God has placed us in, who know increasingly what it means to love the Lord God with all our heart, soul, and mind. We are not to exploit our faculties and gifts for selfish ends, but neither are we to leave them undeveloped. We are to develop them fully and to rejoice in them as gifts from God which enable us to comprehend the glories of our Creator in his many-sided creation, thus more profoundly appreciating the redemptive act of God in Jesus Christ. We squander time and talent when we fail to take them seriously, throwing them away on worthless things. This is to steal from God.

One further way in which we may steal from God involves the abuse of our environment. Christians ought to be actively engaged in the recent, if belated, concern for ecology in our world. The natural environment and its perpetual renewal are gifts of God, and the greatness of these gifts is unmistakably evident despite the fact that the creation was marred by the fall of Adam. Twentieth-century man has, with the horrendous monster of his technology, left the ugly imprint of grimy hands on his environment. The irony of it all is that this desecration of the environment is done in the name of progress. Pollution, however, is about the best example of the attempt to steal from God and its result. God means for the environment to be used and enjoyed. But what God gives freely and lovingly, men greedily snatch and exploit. Why do men behave in such an incredible manner? Because they sincerely believe that to get is to live.

The cult of our society's religion, profit making, needs no justification. It is a self-evident truth, is it not, that a man's life consists in the abundance of things he possesses? Meanwhile man destroys his forests, his lakes and rivers, the animal, plant, and aquatic life. He contaminates the very air he breathes, the food he eats, and the water he drinks. He turns his landscape into mountains of wreckage, his environment into one colossal garbage dump.

In attempting to steal from God, man only brings ruin upon himself. How utterly absurd to steal from the God who delights in giving! It is paradoxical, but true: He who steals from God in the end only steals from himself.

The motif underlying what I have been saying is contained in a single word which I have not yet mentioned. The word is *stewardship*. Unfortunately for many Christians, stewardship is identified solely with the financial support of the institutional church. But this is far too narrow a view of the word. Stewardship, conceived biblically, is all-encompassing. It is not only money that God has entrusted to our stewardship. He has made us stewards of all of His gifts to man, including even the good news of the gospel.

Here is the key to a biblical understanding of the things we have been discussing. Properly speaking, the Christian does not own his possessions; he has only been entrusted with the care of certain things. Existentially he is well aware that even as he came into the world naked, so also will he depart this world naked. The things he has are merely on temporary loan, and consequently he can live lightly in regard to them. He is quite content with what God sends him. This does not mean he is passive. He labors diligently at his job, but like the apostle Paul, he knows how to be abased and how to abound, and how to be content with his circumstances (Phil 4:12, KJV). He knows also that even as God has so richly given to him so also ought his life to be characterized by giving.

It is readily apparent how contradictory the very thought of stealing is to this frame of mind. Stealing is the antithesis of stewardship. Not only does stealing involve the implicit exaltation of the ego, it also involves an exaltation of the intrinsic value of possessions and a depreciation of the worth of individuals. It is hard to imagine results more contradictory to Christianity. The attempt to steal from God—need it be said—also violates the notion of stewardship. There is no need to steal from the one who gives, and the attempt to do so betrays an unfortunate lack of understanding on our part.

The apostle Paul once wrote to the Ephesians, "Let him who steals steal no longer; but rather let him labor, performing with his own hands what is good, in order that he may have something to share with him who has need" (Eph 4:28).

A greater Man than he once said, "It is more blessed to give than to receive" (Ac 20:35).

The Ninth Commandment

STEVEN BARABAS

EXODUS 20:16: *You shall not bear false witness against your neighbor.*

The gift of speech is a divine endowment, bestowed upon man by God as part of the image of God in which he was created. It lifts him far above the animal world. Animals can plan and build, can love and hate, can play and fight, but they cannot speak. Animals have their cities, and their governments, and their stores of food, and even their wars; but while some have rudimentary ways of communicating with each other, they have no words.

Only man can commune with his Creator in words. Only man can share with others his deepest thoughts and highest aspirations. Through words, whether in spoken or written form, we can glorify God, as we do in our hymns and in prayer. We can bring help, comfort, and courage to others in need, but through words we can also bring untold harm and anguish. We can wound; we can stab; we can crush; yes, we can kill. Many a good man's name has been ruined by lying words. Many a soul created in God's image has been murdered by words—spoken or written.

The ninth commandment has to do with the misuse of the tongue—using it to injure another by lying about or misrepresenting him. The commandment is not limited to bearing false witness against another in a court of law, although that is undoubtedly included in it.

79

Like almost all of the Ten Commandments, it is stated in the form of a prohibition—"You shall not bear false witness against your neighbor." We must not, however, assume that God is satisfied if only we refrain from doing a wrong. He requires right action and right motives. I once heard the famous Yale professor of English literature, William Lyons Phelps, tell about meeting a mother who boasted to him about her wonderful son. He did not drink or smoke or play cards or gamble or dance or keep bad company. The professor listened patiently to her and then asked, "Lady, what *does* your son do?"

Because of the importance of the tongue, God has much to say about it in His Word. The very first recorded conversation in the Bible, in Genesis 3, illustrates the harmful way the tongue may be used. The serpent persuaded Eve that God was a liar and a cheat who was trying to keep from her and Adam all that would make them happy. The disastrous consequences of the fall are the result of a terrible misuse of the tongue. The serpent bore false witness against God.

First, how we use our tongue shows what we are inside. When a doctor sees a patient, one of the first things he usually says is, "Let me see your tongue." The patient's physical condition is often indicated by the state of his tongue. Jesus said that what a person says is evidence of what he is inside. "The mouth speaks that which fills the heart" (Mt 12:31) . What a person says is simply the overflow of his heart.

Words are incarnate thoughts. They are a revelation of character. The language of our lips is dictated by what we think and feel—and are. The utterance of the tongue, Jesus says, is a sure indication of the actual state of the heart. Socrates put it in different words but meant the same thing when he said, "Speak that I may see thee."

If there is hatred in the heart, it will reveal itself in your speech. If there is jealousy or envy or resentment, your words will betray that fact. If you lie about another person, it shows that in your heart there are sinful emotions—envy, jealousy, hatred, or perhaps even murder. And remember that Jesus said that in the eyes of God murder is not limited to ending another person's life; it is also bitter hatred of another.

God says that a person's spiritual condition is indicated by the use of his tongue. James 1:26 says, "If any one thinks himself to be religious, and yet does not bridle his tongue . . . this man's religion is worthless." You say that you are a Christian. Are you? God says that if any man thinks he is a Christian and does not bridle his tongue, this man's Christianity is a fraud.

The Word of God also teaches us that our tongue shapes our character. Words not only reveal character, they shape and mold character. Your words reveal what you will be like as a person next year, in five years, in ten years. James 3:6 says that the tongue defiles the whole body. Socrates, in the *Apology,* says, "False words are not only evil in themselves, but they infect the soul with evil."

Let us see how this works out. If when we are tempted to criticize another, we hold our tongue, we are on the way to a mastery of the spirit of criticism. If, however, we yield to the temptation, we will become more and more critical until we can no longer free ourselves. We become prisoners of the spirit of criticism. If when we are tempted to malign another person, we check the temptation and pray for him instead, we develop in us the spirit of truth, compassion and love. The seventeenth century writer, Francis Quarles, said, "Give not thy tongue too great liberty lest it take thee prisoner."

The great Baptist preacher, F. B. Meyer, in one of his messages told how he overcame the spirit of jealousy. After becoming world-renowned as a Bible conference speaker, he was alarmed to find himself becoming jealous and critical. At the Northfield Bible Conference where he had spoken year after year, Meyer observed that a young new speaker seemed to be more popular than he was. This was hard for him to take, but he knew it was wrong. He overcame his jealous emotions, he tells us, by praying daily for that young man, G. Campbell Morgan.

When we try to influence others with words, whether for good or for evil, we shape our own character. We become like what we try to make other people become. That is one of the laws of the kingdom of God that is inwrought in the very constitution of our human nature. There is no escaping it.

A third important lesson the Word of God teaches us about the use of the tongue is that it directs and shapes the lives of others for good or ill.

God says in Proverbs 18:21, "Death and life are in the power of the tongue." This is to me one of the most solemnizing verses in the Bible. I still remember how shocked I was when I came across it for the first time. God says that the tongue has awesome power to bring life or to bring death.

The tongue has power to bring death to others. Let us see what Scripture has to say about this. The author of Proverbs 25:15 says, "A soft tongue breaks the bone." And again he says, "There is one who speaks rashly like the thrusts of a sword" (Pr 12:18). Have you ever seen someone stabbed in the back by the sword thrust of someone's lying tongue? Of some people who lived in Jeremiah's time the prophet says, "Their tongue is a deadly arrow" (Jer. 9:8), and "They bend their tongue like their bow" (Jer 9:3). The psalmist prays, "Hide me from the secret counsel of evil doers, From the tumult of those who do iniquity, Who have sharpened their tongue like a sword; they aimed bitter speech as their arrow, To shoot from concealment at the blameless; Suddenly they shoot at him, and do not fear" (Ps 64:2-4). James says that the tongue, though small in size, has tremendous influence over human lives. "We put the bits in the horses' mouths so that they may obey us, we direct their entire body as well. Behold, the ships also, though they are so great and are driven by strong winds, are still directed by a very small rudder, wherever the inclination of the pilot desires" (Ja 3:3-4).

An illustration of the harm the tongue can do to others is the story of the ten spies who by their unbelieving, discouraging words dissuaded the Israelites from entering the promised land. It was God's intention that the Israelites enter the promised land soon after they left Sinai, and they might very well have done so if ten of the twelve men sent to spy out the land had not frightened them so much with their stories of giants in the land that they refused to believe that God would enable them to possess it. As a result, all of them except the two believing spies, Caleb and Joshua, died in the wilderness, some wandering around in it as many as forty years.

A few years ago I had an exceptionally brilliant student in one of my classes. When the fall semester opened, I missed him; and one day I asked the dean of students where he was. The dean told me that he was asked not to come back because of the harmful influence he had over the other students. He had a very persuasive tongue with which he poisoned the souls of so many others that he was not allowed to come back for his senior year. What a tragedy!

James 3:9-10 says, "With it [our tongue] we bless our Lord and Father; and with it we curse men, who have been made in the likeness of God; from the same mouth come both blessing and cursing. My brethren, these things ought not to be this way."

We talk and sing a great deal nowadays about loving one another. Are we really sincere? Can we love someone and at the same time stab or murder him spiritually with our tongue?

But the tongue also has power to bring life to others. Scripture teaches us that the tongue is to be used to glorify God and bring spiritual help to others.

The psalmist gives us an example of how the tongue is to be used when he says, "Come and hear, all who fear God, And I will tell of what He has done for my soul. I cried unto Him with my mouth . . . God has heard; He has given heed to the voice of my prayer" (Ps 66:16-17, 19) ; "My tongue also will utter Thy righteousness all day long" (Ps 71:24). The prophet Isaiah, realizing the spiritual weakness of many Israelites in his time, urges the spiritually strong to "Encourage the exhausted, and strengthen the feeble." Say to those who are of a fearful heart, "Take courage" (Is 35:3-4) , and a little later he says, "Each one helps his neighbors, And says to his brother, 'Be strong' " (Is 41:6). Of his own ministry he said, "The Lord God has given Me the tongue of disciples, That I may know how to sustain the weary with a word" (Is 50:4).

The writer of Proverbs says, "A soothing tongue is a tree of life" (Pr 15:4), and "The tongue of the wise brings healing" (Pr 12:18).

The apostle Paul writes to the Christians at Ephesus, "Let no unwholesome word proceed from your mouth, but only such a word as is good for edification according to the need of the moment, that it may give grace to those who hear" (Eph 4:29).

One of the best illustrations of the proper use of the tongue is told in connection with the friendship of David and Jonathan. Although David had been anointed to be the next king of Israel by Samuel in a private ceremony some years before, Saul sought his life, pursuing him like a wild animal in the mountain caves of Judah. David must have been very discouraged, and it was then we are told that "Jonathan, Saul's son, arose and went to David at Horesh, and encouraged him in God. Thus he said to him, Do not be afraid, because the hand of Saul my father shall not find you, and you will be king over Israel and I will be next to you; and Saul my father knows that also" (1 Sa 23:16-17). How long has it been since you encouraged some weary, discouraged Christian friend?

The turning point in the life of John Bunyan came when one day he chanced to overhear three or four poor women sitting at a door in the sun, talking about the things of God.

"Their talk," he says, "was about a new birth, the work of God on their hearts . . . They talked of how God had visited their souls with His love in the Lord Jesus and with what words and promises they had been refreshed and comforted and supported against the temptations of the devil. And methought they spake as if joy did make them speak; they spake with such pleasantness of Scripture language . . . that they were to me as if they had found a new world." And he goes on to say that as he went about his work as a tinker, mending the pots and pans of the neighborhood, that their talk and discourse went with him. What would have happened to John Bunyan if those women had been talking about their neighbors or criticizing their minister and their church? Do you see why God says that death and life are in the power of the tongue?

Let us never forget the words of Jesus that at the judgment we shall have to answer to God for the words we speak. "I say to you, that every careless word that men shall speak, they shall render account for it in the day of judgment. For by your words you shall be justified, and by your words you shall be condemned" (Mt 12:36-37).

James says that it is difficult, indeed impossible, for us to control our tongues by our own will power. "For every species of beasts and birds, of reptiles and creatures of the sea, is tamed, and has been tamed by the human race. But no one can tame the tongue; it is a restless evil and full of deadly poison" (Jas 3:7-8).

In view of these facts, it would be good if every day we would vow with the psalmist, "I will guard my ways, That I may not sin with my tongue; I will guard my mouth as with a muzzle" (Ps 39:1), and if we would pray as he did, "Set a guard, O Lord, over my mouth; Keep watch over the door of my lips" (Ps 141:3), and "Let the words of my mouth and the meditation of my heart Be acceptable in Thy sight, O Lord, my rock and my redeemer" (Ps 19:14).

The Tenth Commandment

DONALD LAKE

EXODUS 20:17: *You shall not covet your neighbor's house; you shall not covet your neighbor's wife or his male servant or his female servant or his ox or his donkey or anything that belongs to your neighbor.*

> And all the people perceived the thunder and the lightning flashes and the sound of the trumpet and the mountain smoking; and when the people saw it, they trembled and stood at a distance. Then they said to Moses, "Speak to us yourself and we will listen; but let not God speak to us, lest we die." And Moses said to the people, "Do not be afraid; for God has come in order to test you, and in order that the fear of Him may remain with you, so that you may not sin" (Ex 20:18-20).

Although the sin of coveting can be said to lie behind many expressions of evil in early biblical history, not until the time of Achan do we find an explicit reference to man's violation of the tenth commandment.

> So Achan answered Joshua and said, "Truly, I have sinned against the Lord, the God of Israel, and this is what I did; when I saw among the spoil a beautiful mantle from Shinar and two hundred shekels of silver and a bar of gold fifty shekels in weight, then I coveted them and took them; and behold, they are concealed in the earth inside my tent with the silver underneath it" (Jos 7:20-21).

The defeat of the Israelites at Ai by a weaker, lesser foe was due to the sin of coveting. Psalms 34:12 is a rare instance in which the term *coveting* is used in a positive sense. "Who is the man who desires life, And loves [covets] length of days that he may see good?" The writer of Proverbs contrasts the wicked man with the righteous when he says, "All day long he [the wicked] is craving [coveting], while the righteous gives and does not hold back" (Pr 21:26). When the prophet Isaiah wanted to explain the reasons why God's judgment was falling upon God's people, he said, "Because of the iniquity of his unjust gain [covetousness] I was angry and struck him; I hid my face and was angry, and he went on turning away [backsliding], in the way of his heart" (Is 57:17). And when Micah tried to discover the reasons for social injustice and poverty in his day, he found that the underlying sin was covetousness! In Micah 2:2 he said, "They covet fields and then seize them, and houses, and take them away. They rob a man and his house, a man and his inheritance." When the Lord Jesus entered into a debate with the Pharisees over the question of ritual cleansing, he pointed out to his opponents that what defiles a man is not the externals, but the internal condition of a man's heart.

> "That which proceeds out of the man, that is what defiles the man. For from within, out of the heart of men, proceed the evil thoughts and fornications, thefts, murders, adulteries, deeds of coveting and wickedness, as well as deceit, sensuality, envy, slander, pride and foolishness. All these evil things proceed from within and defile the man." (Mk 7:20-23).

In another episode a young man came to Jesus saying, "Teacher, tell my brother to divide the family inheritance with me." Jesus gave a surprising response. He said that it was not His responsibility to get involved in domestic disputes over inheritance, but "beware, and be on your guard against every form of greed [covetousness]; for not even when one has an abundance does his life consist of his possessions" (Lk 12:13-15). Then He gave them the parable of the rich fool. The man's fields brought forth an abundant harvest. The man pondered, "What shall I do?" Then a brilliant idea came into his mind: "I will tear down my barns and build larger ones, and there I will store all my grain and my goods. And I will say to my soul, 'Soul, you have many goods laid up for many years to come; take your ease, eat, drink and be merry.' But God said to him, 'You fool! This very night your soul is required of you; and now who will own what you have prepared?' So is the man who lays up treasure for himself, and is not rich toward God" (Lk 12:16-21).

When the apostle Paul met with the Ephesian elders on his last journey to Jerusalem he reminded them of his own conduct in their midst.

> I have coveted no one's silver or gold or clothes. You yourselves know that these hands ministered to my own needs and to the men who were with me. In everything I showed you that by working hard in this manner you must help the weak and remember the words of the Lord Jesus, that He Himself said, "It is more blessed to give than to receive" (Ac 20:33-35).

Paul gave this saying of Jesus, not contained in the gospels, as an illustration of the selflessness of Christ, and a selflessness which Paul demonstrated by example for the Ephesian Christians. Further, when Paul wanted to describe the moral degeneration of the pagan, heathen world, he said they were "filled with all unrighteousness, wickedness, greed [covetousness], malice; full of envy, murder, strife, deceit, malice; they are gossips" (Ro 1:29).

Paul describes the transformation that comes into the Christian life in the book of Ephesians when he says, "But do not let immorality or any impurity or greed [covetousness] even be named among you, as is proper among saints. . . . For this you know with certainty, that no immoral or impure person or covetous man, who is an idolater, has an inheritance in the kingdom of Christ and God" (Eph. 5:3, 5) . Again in Colossians 3:5 Paul states: "Therefore consider the members of your earthly body as dead to immorality, impurity, passion, evil desire, and greed, which amounts to idolatry." In a passage which sounds like a contemporary commentary on our times, James puts the question to his audience, "What is the source of quarrels and conflicts among you? Is not the source your pleasures that wage war in your members? You lust and do not have; so you commit murder. And you are envious [covetous] and cannot obtain; so you fight and quarrel. You do not have because you do not ask. You ask and do not receive, because you ask with the wrong motives, so that you may spend it on your pleasures" (Ja 4:1-3) .

Finally, in 1 John the Word of God contrasts the Christian, who lives according to the will of God, with the worldly man who allows lust and covetousness to control his character.

> Do not love the world, nor the things in the world. If anyone loves the world, the love of the Father is not in him. For all that is in the world, the lust of the flesh and the lust of the eyes and the boastful pride of life, is not from the Father, but is from the world. And the world is passing away, and also its lusts; but the one who does the will of God abides forever (1 Jn 2:15-17) .

Now we need to consider the relevant questions this commandment addresses to us today. First of all, it raises the question of priorities. All of the commandments seem to point back to the first one: "You shall have no other gods before Me" (Ex 20:3) . When the apostle Paul says that the Christian is not to be dominated or controlled by covetousness, he points out that coveting is idolatry (Eph 5:3, 5) . When our lives are controlled by lust and coveting, we have our priorities wrong.

Actually there is a double side to this issue of spiritual priorities. On the one hand, when we covet we place things or people in God's place. That is sin—the sin of idolatry. On the other hand, to covet means to desire for ourselves what belongs to God. And this raises the second issue concerning the tenth commandment: the question of possessions. The Christian is first of all a steward. If you have read the New Testament description of the Christian, you have no doubt been impressed with the fact that the Christian is consistently described as a servant and steward. In no sense can the Christian claim to be the lord and master of his own destiny. And that not only applies to everything he has under his charge but his own life also!

In another sense this commandment is clearly related to the eighth commandment, the commandment or prohibition against stealing. It is interesting that in Stamm and Andrews'[1] recent work on the Ten Commandments, they divide the first commandment and put the eighth and tenth commandments together. And there is indeed a legitimate sense in which these commandments do belong together.

Again we need to see the double side of the possession issue as it relates to the tenth commandment. Do we really own anything? Is there really the right of private property, or does this commandment say that all of us are stewards? Everything we have has been entrusted to us by God, and we cannot claim or possess it for our own. The prohibition against coveting may not be meant to imply that even our neighbor owns something which by coveting we intentionally desire to steal or possess, but it rather implies that both what we have and what our neighbor has belongs to God. God the Father, Lord of creation and history, owns and controls everything! Therefore we violate and encroach upon God's prerogative when we begin to covet something and fail to see that whatever we have has been given us only as a trust, not as a personal possession. We are not owners; we are stewards (Lk 16:1-13; 1 Co 4:1-2; Titus 1:7.) To covet or desire another man's stewardship is to deny the Lord who entrusted the man with the stewardship in the first place!

There is, however, another side to the question of possessions. We should not fail to sense the contemporary relevance of the tenth commandment to the great economic issues of today. Considerable discussion is being carried on within the church today over the relationship of Christianity to capitalism and communism or socialism. I believe that the tenth commandment has a word to say to these discussions. If I understand the commandment correctly, it teaches personal stewardship but not collective stewardship. Although the commandment is not an endorsement of *laissez-faire* capitalism, it is clearly condemnation of all collectivist societies in which personal stewardship is negated. The voluntary sharing of the early apostolic church does not seem to be an exception to this. Biblically speaking, stewardship is always a personal responsibility, and even the spontaneity of the *agape* sharing in Acts did not stand the test of endurance. It is not accidental, at least to my own thinking, that communism— dialectical materialism—is both materialistic and atheistic. The tenth commandment with its implied lordship of God rules every materialistic ideology out of bounds for any Christian. So-called Christian socialism may appear appealing with its call to benevolence, but it lacks the realism of the tenth commandment.

Finally, the tenth commandment raises the question of the principles of Christian economics. There are three economic levels in life. The lowest economic level is the level of necessity. Here the law of life rules. This is the level where one is forced to ask: what does it take to survive in terms of food, clothing, and shelter? But there is a higher and second economic level, the level of expedience. Here the law of convenience and efficiency operates. The question this level asks is what does it take to be comfortable and efficient? There is, however, a third and highest level, the level of luxury, where the law of enjoyment provides the guiding norm. And it is only in affluent societies that this third level becomes even a possibility. It is both an option and a problem in American society.

In our abundant, affluent society, the Christian is confronted with the question, What shall I do with my surplus? There are two options open to the non-Christian. One is the option of indulgence. Since the non-Christian assumes that he owns himself and his surplus, and that he can use it however he wants, he may choose to live an indulgent life. The indulgent man may not worship his money and wealth; for him money is only a means to secure such things as pleasure, clothes, and cars. He asks, what do I want? What do I see? What do others have? What's new? What's different? There is a hedonistic element in human nature that would lead all of us to live for pleasure. The non-Christian may also be idolatrous. He can be a man who is mad over money and possessions, who makes wealth his goal and god! Covetousness is idolatry!

Now, the Christian also has two options open to him, provided he lives in an affluent society. He can affirm the monastic vows of poverty, chastity, and obedience. If he makes more than it takes to live, he automatically gives it away. He consciously and willfully lives on the level of necessity. Few Christians have found this to be the most practical and scriptural answer to the problem of economic surplus.

A more biblical, theological, realistic, and constructive approach to this problem is the principle of immaterialization. How does it work? When my needs have been met and when I have secured those items that make my responsibilities easier and more efficient and there is still a surplus, I can save the surplus, invest it to earn additional sums, or I can use it for some personal enjoyment, provided I do not worship the enjoyment or make it an end in itself. The opportunity to save or invest with interest can be understood and defended as another means of stewardship. And if God owns me, He also owns my investments and banking or saving's accounts, too. God commends the wise steward in Matthew 25:14-30.

But what about the use of this surplus for my own personal enjoyment? Can that be rationalized? Is it possible for the sincere Christian to enjoy, but not worship, life with its comforts? I think it is! We need to remember what Paul admonishes: "Instruct those who are rich in this present world not to be conceited or to fix their hope on the uncertainty of riches, but on God, who richly supplies us with all things to enjoy" (1 Ti 6:17). It is significant that Paul did not say, regarding the rich, what Christ said to the rich young ruler: "Go and sell all you possess, and give it to the poor, and you shall have treasure in heaven" (Mk 10:21). I personally consider the wealth of this rich land a divine blessing and an opportunity, not simply to give away, but to use rightfully for one's personal enjoyment as well as to relieve the physical needs of the disadvantaged of the world. I believe that the Spirit-filled life is to be one of physical and material enjoyment as well as spiritual joy.

What then is the principle of immaterialization? It involves two key concepts: (1) it is spiritually permissible for the Christian to enjoy whatever economic surplus the Lord has provided, provided the surplus was not received either as a violation of the laws of God or the laws of men; (2) all enjoyments must be matched by an equal gift to the work of Christ. Here is a simple illustration: suppose I desire to purchase a beautiful picture for a room in my home. The picture is neither necessary nor expedient, but it would add to the beauty of my home. If the picture costs fifty dollars, the principle of immaterialization requires that I match the fifty-dollar-picture purchase with a fifty-dollar donation to the work of Christ. This principle results in a twofold benefit. First, it qualifies all enjoyments by requiring that they be justified on spiritual grounds; and second, my personal enjoyment is always matched by a benefit to the work of Christ. If I cannot match my personal purchase for enjoyment sake with an equal contribution to the work of Christ, then I cannot purchase the item for personal enjoyment.

Obviously, every man's situation is different. I am the parent of a child born with a serious heart ailment. In the management of my own finances, I am responsible for providing the best available medical care I can afford. Each Christian will have to apply the economic principles to his own situation. But I have found these to be helpful, and they may be of service to you as well.

This analysis would be incomplete without noticing three practical implications contained in this commandment. First, most commentators on this tenth commandment note the distinctive position assigned to the wife. The implication here is that the woman stands apart from and above one's household and one's other personal property. We need not labor the point, but a careful examination of the role and relationship of women in the Bible would correct a lot of misconceptions about the status of women, especially the injustice done to Paul's teaching. Second, one cannot help but notice the relationship between this commandment and the tendency to pattern our lives after our society and our peers. What determines our life-styles? Are we simply adopting the style, dress, and behavior pattern of our peer group? We can violate the intention and spirit of this commandment by a hankering after the fashions of contemporary society! The Christian is called to be conformed to the image of Christ (Ro 8:29-30; 12:1-2). And third, this commandment, addressed to us in our situation, calls attention to the social dimensions of the commandments.

It should disturb us a great deal that much of the social thrust of the church is based upon a covetous desire to be like those in the suburbs. We cannot consistently condemn the affluent while at the same time fashion our welfare programs on a covetous design to be where they are: in the suburbs! One's motivation in life must be to fulfill the will of God in my historical existence, not the striving to be financially like the rich. Although the Christian needs to be warned that his life does not consist in the abundance of his possessions, we commit the sin of coveting when we make material prosperity the norm of our welfare programming. This in no way implies a reduction in the Christian's social concern. The Christian's responsibility for the poor needs no further documentation than the abundant biblical texts on the subject (Pr 14: 21, 31; Jer 2:34; Eze 16:49; Mt 11:5; Ro 15:26; Gal 2:10; 6:10). But the Christian who has been born or providentially forced into a lower economic level must not allow the lust or desire for worldly possessions to replace the will of God as the motivating force of his life. Every Christian must strive in his economic existence to ask what this Word of God, this tenth commandment, means to him. The tenth commandment is addressed to management and employees! It is a Word of God addressed to us in every issue of labor and wage demands. It confronts us with a divine responsibility to live under the concreteness of the will of God.

NOTES

1. J. J. Stamm and M. E. Andrew, *Ten Commandments in Recent Research, Studies in Biblical Theology,* Second Series, no. 2 (Naperville, Ill.: Allensons, 1967).